T0316602

Cambridge Elements ≡

Elements in Research Methods for Developmental Science
edited by
Brett Laursen
Florida Atlantic University

ALGORITHMS FOR MEASUREMENT INVARIANCE TESTING

Contrasts and Connections

Veronica T. Cole
Wake Forest University

Conor H. Lacey
Wake Forest University

CAMBRIDGE
UNIVERSITY PRESS

CAMBRIDGE
UNIVERSITY PRESS

Shaftesbury Road, Cambridge CB2 8EA, United Kingdom

One Liberty Plaza, 20th Floor, New York, NY 10006, USA

477 Williamstown Road, Port Melbourne, VIC 3207, Australia

314–321, 3rd Floor, Plot 3, Splendor Forum, Jasola District Centre,
New Delhi – 110025, India

103 Penang Road, #05–06/07, Visioncrest Commercial, Singapore 238467

Cambridge University Press is part of Cambridge University Press & Assessment,
a department of the University of Cambridge.

We share the University's mission to contribute to society through the pursuit of
education, learning and research at the highest international levels of excellence.

www.cambridge.org
Information on this title: www.cambridge.org/9781009454179

DOI: 10.1017/9781009303408

First published 2023

A catalogue record for this publication is available from the British Library

ISBN 978-1-009-45417-9 Hardback
ISBN 978-1-009-30338-5 Paperback
ISSN 2632-9964 (online)
ISSN 2632-9956 (print)

Additional resources for this publication at www.cambridge.org/cole-Lacey

Algorithms for Measurement Invariance Testing

Contrasts and Connections

Elements in Research Methods for Developmental Science

DOI: 10.1017/9781009303408
First published online: December 2023

Veronica T. Cole
Wake Forest University

Conor H. Lacey
Wake Forest University

Author for correspondence: Veronica T. Cole, colev@wfu.edu

Abstract: Latent variable models are a powerful tool for measuring many of the phenomena in which developmental psychologists are often interested. If these phenomena are not measured equally well among all participants, this would result in biased inferences about how they unfold throughout development. In the absence of such biases, measurement invariance is achieved; if this bias is present, differential item functioning (DIF) would occur. This Element introduces the testing of measurement invariance/DIF through nonlinear factor analysis. After introducing models which are used to study these questions, the Element uses them to formulate different definitions of measurement invariance and DIF. It also focuses on different procedures for locating and quantifying these effects. The Element finally provides recommendations for researchers about how to navigate these options to make valid inferences about measurement in their own data.

Keywords: differential item functioning, measurement invariance, measurement bias, latent variable models, item response theory

ISBNs: 9781009454179 (HB), 9781009303385 (PB), 9781009303408 (OC)
ISSNs: 2632-9964 (online), 2632-9956 (print)

Contents

1 Algorithms for Measurement Invariance Testing: Contrasts and Connections   1

2 Latent Variable Models   3

3 What is Measurement Invariance? What is DIF?   12

4 Codifying Measurement Noninvariance and Differential Item Functioning in Different Latent Variable Frameworks   20

5 Models for Measurement Noninvariance and Differential Item Functioning   25

6 Consequences of Measurement Noninvariance and Differential Item Functioning   47

7 Detecting Measurement Noninvariance and Differential Item Functioning   51

8 Recommendations for Best Practices   69

References   74

1 Algorithms for Measurement Invariance Testing: Contrasts and Connections

There are many reasonable places to start in an introduction to the study of measurement invariance and differential item functioning (DIF). Though it may seem overly broad, we can start by stating the goal of measurement in general. If we administer a set of items, it is typically because we assume that they indirectly assess some underlying quality which cannot be easily observed. These quantities are typically referred to as latent variables, and they represent some of the constructs in which developmental scientists are often most interested.

The study of measurement invariance and differential item functioning concerns the question of whether this measurement process unfolds equally well for all participants. If features of individual participants – which often include demographic variables such as age, sex, gender, or race, but can be any person- or context-specific quantity – are associated with different relations between latent variables and their observable measures, our inferences about this latent variable will be biased. Moreover, when we aim to compare participants who differ in these dimensions, we may make erroneous conclusions.

An example of a recent analysis of DIF helps to understand the issues at hand. Anxious symptoms are quite common among children on the autism spectrum, and it is therefore critical to have measures of anxiety that function well in this population. One recent study (Schiltz & Magnus, 2021) analyzed how well a parent-report measure, the Screen for Child Anxiety Related Disorders (SCARED; Birmaher et al., 1997), measures symptoms of anxiety disorders in a sample of $N = 198$ children on the autism spectrum (mean age = 11.18 years). Among other covariates, the authors examined the effects of children's social functioning, as measured by the Social Communication Questionnaire (SCQ; Rutter et al., 2003), on the link between SCARED scores and the latent variables they aim to represent, in this case five dimensions of anxiety (panic disorder, generalized anxiety disorder, separation anxiety, social anxiety, school avoidance). They found that certain social anxiety items – particularly "feels shy with people he/she does not know well" and "is shy" – were less commonly endorsed among parents whose children showed high SCQ scores, regardless of the child's level of social anxiety. This last portion of the findings is critical: the fact that SCQ score was negatively related to endorsement of these items *even after controlling for the latent variable, social anxiety*, means that children's social functioning may have a negatively biasing effect on their parents' reports of their social anxiety. In other words, if a parent rates their child highly in these social anxiety symptoms on the SCARED, this may reflect deficits in the child's social functioning, rather than the child's experience of anxiety. Studying measurement invariance and DIF in these items is one way to avoid making such an error.

1.0.1 Terminology and History

The study of measurement bias has a rich intellectual history, with many different researchers addressing these issues at many different times in the past century (Millsap, 2011). The complexity of this landscape has led to a somewhat challenging terminological issue: the terms *measurement invariance* and *differential item functioning* effectively refer to the same concept in different ways. In general, researchers using structural equation modeling (SEM), particularly confirmatory factor analysis (CFA), developed the term *measurement invariance* to describe an assumption: that the items in a given test measure the latent variable equally for all individuals (Meredith, 1993; Millsap, 2011; Putnick et al., 2016). At the same time, research arising mostly from the item response theory (IRT) tradition uses the term *differential item functioning*, often abbreviated DIF, to describe cases in which this assumption is violated: that is, items or sets thereof in which measurement parameters differ across participants (Holland & Thayer, 1986; Osterlind & Everson, 2009; Thissen et al., 1993). For readers interested in the long history of the study of measurement invariance and DIF, which extends back over a century, are referred to one historical review (Millsap & Meredith, 2007), which provides a fascinating overview of this literature.

However, for the purposes of this Element, there are two important things to note. First is that the study of DIF and measurement invariance have largely come together in the past two decades, perhaps due to the wider adoption of models (e.g., nonlinear factor models, discussed in the next section) which can be extended to accommodate many models within SEM and IRT (Bauer, 2017; Knott & Bartholomew, 1999; Millsap, 2011; Skrondal & Rabe-Hesketh, 2004). The concordance between these two traditions' treatment of the same phenomenon has been noted many times before (Reise et al., 1993; Stark et al., 2004, 2006), and contemporary modeling tools have been useful in helping researchers to unify these two perspectives. The second thing to note is that the terms will be used interchangeably throughout this Element. In general, measurement invariance will mostly be referred to when discussing an assumption (e.g., ensuring that different types of measurement invariance are satisfied), whereas DIF will be used to describe an effect (e.g., DIF effects were found for some items in this test). However, some slippage between the terms is unavoidable, given that – as we will see shortly – the two refer to virtually identical concepts.

For more information about the terminology used in this Element, readers are referred to the Glossary in Table 1.

1.0.2 Organization of This Element

The main goals of this Element are to give developmental scientists as comprehensive a summary of measurement invariance and DIF research as possible, with the goal of helping them to incorporate the theory and practice of this research area into their own work. We begin with as complete a description of latent variable models as possible. The Element aims to provide a mathematical framework for the specific discussion of exactly what measurement invariance and DIF are. We will then mathematically define the types of DIF effects one might encounter, as well as different fields' frameworks for studying DIF in general. Readers already familiar with the different types of measurement invariance (e.g., configural, metric, scalar) and DIF (e.g., uniform, nonuniform) may wish to skip this portion, particularly if they are already familiar with nonlinear latent variable models.

The second portion of this Element concerns the different extensions of the nonlinear factor model which can be used to test the assumption of measurement invariance, or detect and account for DIF. First, we discuss the two main modeling frameworks for addressing these questions, with an eye toward comparing and contrasting different fields' and models' definitions of DIF. We then move on to an exploration of different algorithms used to locate DIF, with a similar goal of examining differences and similarities between different fields. We will end with a set of recommendations for how to incorporate the study of DIF into one's measurement-related research.

2 Latent Variable Models

In order to formulate what measurement invariance is, we must first introduce latent variable models. Most of the models in which measurement invariance is considered fall under the heading of nonlinear factor analysis (Bauer & Hussong, 2009; Knott & Bartholomew, 1999; Skrondal & Rabe-Hesketh, 2004), a broad framework which encompasses most CFA and IRT models. Critically, although this section aims to comprehensively introduce latent variable models, including the nonlinear factor model, it should not be the reader's first introduction to either latent variable models or the generalized linear modeling framework. If either of those are new to the reader, it is suggested that they review a tutorial on factor analysis (e.g., Hoyle, 1995) or logistic regression and the generalized linear model in general (e.g., Hosmer Jr et al., 2013; McCullagh & Nelder, 2019). Those wishing for a comprehensive introduction to nonlinear

Table 1 Glossary of terms used throughout the Element

Term	Definition
alignment	An approximate method of estimating DIF effects which aims to minimize differences between groups in intercept and slope parameters in the context of a multiple-groups model.
approximate methods	A set of methods, encompassing alignment and regularization, which use penalized estimation to minimize the number of small DIF effects found.
configural invariance	The most basic form of measurement invariance, which requires that the number of factors and patterns of loadings is the same across groups.
differential item functioning (DIF)	Differences between participants in the measurement parameters for a particular item. Essentially the relational opposite of measurement invariance – that is, a model with DIF lacks measurement invariance.
effect size	For the purposes of this Element, the magnitude of a DIF effect either in terms of the differences in parameters or implied scores.
factor scores	Estimates generated from a factor model of each individual participant's level of the latent variable.
focal group	In a multiple-groups model, the group for which differences in measurement parameters are of interest; compared to a reference group. Note that, absent substantive hypotheses, "focal" and "reference" groups can just be referred to by number (e.g., groups 1, 2, and 3).
likelihood ratio test	An inferential test which compares the fit of one model to another, nested model. For the purposes of this Element, to test the hypothesis that a model with certain DIF or impact parameters fits better than one without them.

measurement invariance	Equality between participants in measurement parameters, either for a single item or an entire test. Essentially the relational opposite of DIF – that is, a model with DIF lacks measurement invariance.
metric invariance	A form of measurement invariance which requires that factor loadings are equal across participants. Sometimes referred to as "weak metric invariance."
multiple-groups model	For the purposes of this Element, a way to formulate DIF which treats DIF as between-group differences in parameter values.
nonuniform DIF	Differences across participants in an item which are not constant across all levels of the latent variable. Typically codified as differences between item loadings.
pre-estimation approaches	For the purposes of this Element, methods of determining the presence and magnitude of DIF effects which do not require a model to be estimated.
reference group	In a multiple-groups model, the group to which the focal group is compared in terms of measurement parameters. Note that, absent substantive hypotheses, "focal" and "reference" groups can just be referred to by number (e.g., groups 1, 2, and 3).
regression-based	For the purposes of this Element, a way to formulate DIF which treats measurement parameters as outcomes in a regression. Contrasted with multiple-groups model.
regularization	An approximate method of estimating DIF effects which penalizes DIF effects in the estimation of a factor model, with the goal of retaining only those effects that are meaningful.

factor analysis are referred to other work which covers this topic extensively (Knott & Bartholomew, 1999; Skrondal & Rabe-Hesketh, 2004).

Although we aim to present measurement invariance in an accessible way, a substantial number of equations in this section are unavoidable. Our hope is that, with some exposure to latent variable models and the generalized linear modeling framework, readers will be able to follow along with this section. The equations themselves do not require more than the above prerequisites (at least some prior exposure to latent variables and regression models outside of linear regression) to understand. Readers familiar with the contents of this section may wish to skim it to get the notation which will be used later on.

2.1 The Common Factor Model

Assume that we have a sample of N participants, to whom we administer a set of J items. The response of the ith participant ($i = 1, \ldots, N$) to the jth item ($j = 1, \ldots, J$) is denoted y_{ij}. Note that we will refer to y_{ij} as an "item" or a "response variable" interchangeably throughout this text. We assume that the items are measures of a set of M latent variables ($m = 1, \ldots, M$). Each individual has an implicit value of each latent variable, denoted η_{im}. In a typical common factor model, we assume that the items are related to the latent variables as follows:

$$y_{ij} = v_j + \sum_{m=1}^{M} \lambda_{mj}\eta_{im} + \epsilon_{ij}. \tag{1}$$

For each item, v_j is the intercept; this represents the predicted value of y_{ij} for an individual whose value on the latent variable(s) which load on y_{ij} is 0. As with intercepts in linear regression, we can effectively think of it as the overall "level" of the item – we predict that participants will, on average, have high overall levels of v_j regardless of their level of the latent variable. The effect of the latent variable is conveyed by λ_{mj}, the factor loading. As with a slope in a linear regression, for each one-unit shift in the mth latent variable we predict a λ_{mj}-unit shift in the item. Finally, ϵ_{ij} represents the error term, which is subject i's deviation from their predicted value of item j. These error terms are assumed to have a mean of 0, and a variance of σ_j^2. Error terms are generally considered to be uncorrelated across items – that is σ_{hj}, which represents the covariance between the error terms for items h and j, is assumed to be 0.

Latent variables may covary with one another, with an $M \times M$ covariance matrix Φ. Each diagonal element of Φ, here denoted ϕ_m^2, represents the variance of the mth latent variable; off-diagonal elements of the matrix, denoted

ϕ_{nm}, represent the covariance between the mth and nth latent variables. Latent variables may also have their own means; the mean of the mth latent variable is denoted α_m.

Some constraints must be imposed on these parameters in order for the model to be identified. There are two common options. First, we can fix one item's value of v_j to 0 and its value of λ_{mj} to 1 for each latent variable. This item is often referred to as the *reference variable* and, when this approach is used, the latent variable is on the same scale as this item. Alternatively, we could set the variances ϕ_m^2 to 1 and the mean α_m to 0 for all latent variables. In this case, the loading λ_{mj} may now be considered the predicted change in y_{ij} associated with a one-standard deviation shift in the latent variable η_{im}; the intercept v_j may now be considered the predicted value of y_{ij} when all latent variables are at their means. As we will see shortly, assessing measurement invariance involves adding a number of new parameters to the model, which will complicate model identification; this is discussed in detail below.

2.2 Nonlinear Factor Models

The common factor model presented above is the foundation of most psychological researchers' understanding of latent variable models. However, in order for us to understand the relations among different latent variable models, it is necessary to extend it. In particular, the above model assumes that items y_{ij} meet the same general assumptions as the dependent variable in a linear regression. For our purpose, the most problematic of these assumptions is that the residuals of the items are normally distributed. This assumption requires, among other things, that our outcome be continuous, which we know many psychological outcomes are not (even if we erroneously treat them that way). In particular, it is common for us to be working with ordinal items resulting from a Likert scale (e.g., responses ranging from 1 to 5 assessing a participant's agreement with a given statement) or even binary items (e.g., a yes–no response to a question about psychiatric symptoms).

Thus, our discussion of DIF will use a nonlinear factor analysis formulation. Although we will attempt to describe the nonlinear factor analysis formulation, we suggest that this not be the reader's first introduction to nonlinear factor models and generalized linear models more generally, as mentioned above. However, for review, a brief description follows.

The major advantage of nonlinear factor models is that they allow the relation between items and latent variables (i.e., the one expressed in Equation 1) to take a nonlinear form, corresponding to items y_{ij} of different scales. The shift to nonlinear variables requires two major innovations on the model presented above. The first is what is known as a linear predictor, which we denote ω_{ij}, and which is formulated as follows:

$$\omega_{ij} = v_j + \sum_{m=1}^{M} \lambda_{mj}\eta_{im}. \tag{2}$$

Note that this is basically the exact same equation as Equation 1, except without the error term. The purpose of the linear predictor becomes a bit clearer when we introduce the second component of nonlinear factor models, known as the link function. In order to get to our expected value of y_{ij}, we must take our linear predictor ω_{ij} and place it inside the inverse link function. Let us unpack each term in this statement. The expected value of y_{ij} is whatever value we would predict for subject i on item j. For binary items, this is the probability that that particular subject will give a response of 1 (e.g., say "yes" to a yes–no question, get a question correct on a test of ability, endorse a given symptom on a symptom inventory based on their level of the latent variable. We will denote this μ_{ij} (following the notation of Bauer and Hussong (2009)).

As for the inverse link function, let us first define the link function, $g(q)$:

$$g(\mu_{ij}) = \omega_{ij}. \tag{3}$$

To put Equation 3 colloquially, we can define the link function $g(x)$ as "whatever function we apply to the expected value of y_{ij} to get to ω_{ij}." Being that the inverse link function, denoted $g^{-1}(q)$, is the inverse of $g(x)$, it can be colloquially defined as "whatever function we apply to ω_{ij} to get to the expected value of y_{ij}." Note that the function $g(x)$ must be bijective in order to have an inverse.

Mathematically, it is defined as follows:

$$g^{-1}(\omega_{ij}) = \mu_{ij}. \tag{4}$$

Thus, in order to get to μ_{ij}, our expected value for y_{ij}, our model is implicitly estimating the linear predictor ω_{ij} and applying the inverse link function. As far as our choices of link and inverse link functions, they depend on the type of data we are interested in modeling. One reasonable choice for binary data is the logit link function, whose inverse will yield a number between 0 and 1, making it well-suited to modeling a probability. As noted above, when we are working with binary data, the expected value of y_{ij} (μ_{ij}) is the probability that a given individual endorses item y_{ij} – that is, $P(y_{ij} = 1)$. Thus, we will use the logit function to translate μ_{ij} to ω_{ij}, and the inverse of that function to translate ω_{ij} to μ_{ij}. The logit link function is defined as follows:

$$g(\mu_{ij}) = \ln \frac{(\mu_{ij})}{1 - (\mu_{ij})} = \omega_{ij}, \tag{5}$$

where ln denotes the natural logarithm. Conversely, the inverse logit link function is defined as follows:

$$g^{-1}(\omega_{ij}) = \frac{\exp(\omega_{ij})}{1 + \exp(\omega_{ij})} = \mu_{ij}, \tag{6}$$

where $\exp(q)$ is shorthand for e^q. If the reader wishes to see that Equation 6 is indeed the inverse of Equation 5, they may choose a value of μ_{ij}, which can be any number between 0 and 1, and plug it into Equation 5. Then take the value of ω_{ij} obtained from Equation 5 and plug it into Equation 6. This transformation should yield the originally chosen value of μ_{ij}.

Putting it all together, we can now finally formulate how the latent variable itself is related to the expected value of a binary item under a nonlinear factor analysis. Combining the original linear formulation in Equation 2 and the inverse link function in Equation 4 we get the following:

$$\mu_{ij} = \frac{\exp\left(v_j + \sum_{m=1}^{M} \lambda_{mj}\eta_{im}\right)}{1 + \exp\left(v_j + \sum_{m=1}^{M} \lambda_{mj}\eta_{im}\right)}. \tag{7}$$

Note that we have the same exact parameters linking the latent variable η_{im} to the item y_{ij}: intercept v_j and loading λ_{mj}. The difference is that now y_{ij} is related by these parameters to the latent variable through a nonlinear function as opposed to a linear one. If the reader wishes to test this out, an example is given in Table 2, in which we have each individual's values of η_i, ω_{ij}, μ_{ij}, and y_{ij} for pre-set values of λ_{mj} and v_j.

There is one more step to understanding nonlinear factor analysis, and that is defining the probability function. Note that the inverse link function does not give us y_{ij} but its expected value – that is, for a binary item it will not give us a value of y_{ij} (which can only take a value of 0 or 1) but rather μ_{ij}, the probability that y_{ij} will be 1. Notice also that our linear predictor has no error term in it – we have not accounted for any source of randomness or error. Thus, the probability function is what links the expected value μ_{ij} to the value of y_{ij} we ultimately obtain. In the case of binary response variables, we generally assume that y_{ij} follows a Bernoulli distribution with probability μ_{ij}.

Colloquially, this means the following. The variable y_{ij} is random and we don't know whether it will be 0 or 1, but we do know the probability with which it will be 1, and that probability is μ_{ij}. A person with $\mu_{ij} = 0.9$ will most likely give a value of 1, a person with $\mu_{ij} = 0.2$ will most likely give a value of 0, and a person with $\mu_{ij} = 0.5$ is just as likely to give a value of 0 or 1, but any one of these people could theoretically give a value of 0 or 1. Note, for instance, in Table 2, that the observed values of y_{ij} take values of 0 or 1, and may even

Table 2 Example values of latent variables (η_i), linear predictors (ω_{ij}), endorsement probabilities (μ_{ij}), and outcomes (y_{ij}), for a nonlinear factor analysis with $\lambda = 1.5$ and $\nu = 0.25$

ID	η_i	ω_{ij}	μ_{ij}	y_{ij}
1	0.5723	1.1084	0.2482	0
2	−0.0034	0.245	0.4391	1
3	−2.7187	−3.828	0.9787	1
4	−0.6953	−0.793	0.6885	0
5	1.3079	2.2118	0.0987	0
6	−0.9547	−1.182	0.7653	1
7	−1.7034	−2.3051	0.9093	1
8	0.204	0.5559	0.3645	0
9	0.3321	0.7482	0.3212	0
10	0.7218	1.3326	0.2087	0

(as in the case of the 8th observation) take a value of 0 if the probability of endorsing the item is over 0.5.

Once we combine all three of these things – the linear predictor, the link function, and the probability function – we have all the information we need to think about factor analysis, and thus DIF, in a way that encompasses many different types of models across disciplines. For instance, the formulation provided above for binary variables, using an inverse logit function to link the linear predictor to the probability of endorsing an item, is actually the same as the two-parameter logistic model in IRT (Birnbaum, 1969). This model is frequently applied to binary data in an IRT setting.

2.2.1 Extensions to Ordinal Data

The above model will suffice for binary data, but ordinal data requires a slightly more complicated extension of this formulation. A model arising from IRT for ordinal data is known as the graded response model (Samejima, 1997). Like the formulation given in Equation 6, we are modeling probabilities. Given an ordinal item with K categories ($k = 1, \ldots, K$), we model the probability of endorsing category k or lower. For instance, in a three-level item, rather than modeling the probability that a participant endorses option 1, 2, or 3, we model the probability that the participant endorses option 1; option 2 or 1; or option 3, 2, or 1. Note that the probability of endorsing option 3, 2, or 1 is exactly 1 – the participant must endorse one of these three options. So we only model $K-1$ probabilities – in this case, the probability of endorsing option 2 or lower, and the probability of endorsing option 1. Note also that the case of binary data is actually a special case of this model – that is, it is a model with $K = 2$ categories.

Whereas in binary data we used μ_{ij} to represent the probability of endorsing a given item, here we use $E\left(y_{kij}\right)$ to represent the cumulative probability of endorsing category k or lower. In the three-level example just given, thus, every participant would have an implied value of $E\left(y_{1ij}\right)$, the probability of endorsing response option 1, and $E\left(y_{2ij}\right)$, the probability of endorsing response option 2 or response option 1. Each value of $E\left(y_{kij}\right)$ has its own linear predictor, which we will denote ω_{kij}. This linear predictor is given by:

$$\omega_{kij} = \tau_{kj} - \left(v_j + \sum_{m=1}^{M} \lambda_{mj}\eta_{im}\right). \tag{8}$$

The new parameter in this equation, τ_{kj}, is the *threshold* parameter. This parameter represents the value of the latent variable a participant must exceed in order to get a score exceeding k. One critical note is that all possible values of τ_{kj} and the intercept v_j cannot all be identified; one of these values must be fixed. The typical solution is to set the intercept v_j to zero in the event that individual thresholds are estimated. Readers who would like a comprehensive description of the τ_{kj} parameter are referred to the original formulation of the model (Bauer & Hussong, 2009), where it is explained more completely.

2.2.2 A Note about Matrices and Vectors

In many cases it is useful to consider all of the above parameters in terms of matrices or vectors, which contain all of the relevant parameters (e.g., all of the loadings, all of the intercepts) for a given model. It is not critical to understand matrix algebra fully to make this distinction; the important thing to know is that, when we designate a matrix or vector of parameters as invariant or non-invariant, that generally means that we are applying the distinction to all of the relevant parameters. For instance, we can consider the factor loadings, each indexed λ_{jm}, as part of a matrix of dimension $J \times M$, Λ.

If we say that we are testing the invariance of Λ, we mean that we are testing the hypothesis that *all* of the loadings, for all items measuring all factors, are invariant across groups. Similarly, we can place all of the intercepts, individually denoted v_j, into a J-length vector, which we will denote v. If we are using a model for ordinal data with individual thresholds for each response category, we can put these into a $J \times K$ matrix τ. With respect to the distribution of the latent variable itself, we can think of the means of each factor as being stored in the M-length vector α, and the covariance matrix of the latent variables as fitting into the $M \times M$ covariance matrix Φ. We can also refer to the error terms as a $J \times J$ matrix Σ.

Finally, we can even refer to the data itself as a matrix. The entire collection of all of the items for all of the participants, individually denoted y_{ij} for participant i on item j, can simply be referred to as a $N \times J$ matrix Y. Similarly, if we believe that subjects each have their own (unobserved) values of the latent variables, we could consider the $N \times M$ matrix of these latent variable values, individually denoted η_{im} for participant i on latent variable m, η.

Though all of these quantities are different from one another, with some consisting of measurement parameters (i.e., Λ, ν, τ), others consisting of latent variable parameters (i.e., α and Φ), and others not being parameters at all (i.e., Y, η), the point is the same: when we refer to a given condition applying to a matrix or a vector, we mean that the condition applies to all of the individual elements within that matrix or vector. This way of referring to the elements of a matrix or vector will become an important one when we distinguish two different ways of thinking about measurement invariance and DIF, as some methods consider individual parameters, whereas others consider the entire matrix thereof.

3 What is Measurement Invariance? What is DIF?

With the nonlinear factor model defined, we are now able to provide formal definitions of measurement invariance within it. Recall that measurement invariance is thought of as the assumption that the relation between the latent variable and the item is constant across all values of other covariates – these can be demographic variables, such as age, or theory-specific variables, such as SDQ score in our first example. We can define the assumption of measurement invariance mathematically as follows.

$$f\left(y_{ij}|\eta_{im}, x_i\right) = f\left(y_{ij}|\eta_{im}\right). \tag{9}$$

Here the items and latent variable are referred to as y_{ij} and η_{im}, just as before; the new addition is x_i, which represents participant i's value of some variable x_i. Note that we use the term *covariate* to refer to this variable. Other terms which are sometimes used are *background variable* or *predictor*. This covariate can be anything about the participant – gender, age, race, location, and so on. What $f\left(y_{ij}|\eta_{im}\right)$ refers to is the probability distribution of y_{ij}, conditional on η_{im}; that is, it represents the value of the jth item the ith subject will get, based on their value of the latent variable. Similarly, $f\left(y_{ij}|\eta_{im}, x_i\right)$ refers to the

i^{th} subject's value on the item given their value of both the latent variable and the covariate x_i.

What this effectively means is: in the absence of measurement bias on the basis of covariate x_i, there will be no more information about y_{ij} that x_i can give us over and above the latent variable itself. Suppose, for example, that we are trying to determine whether an item (y_{ij}) measuring children's math ability (η_{im}) is free of measurement bias on the basis of gender (x_i). If there is no measurement bias, then a girl and a boy who each have the same value of η_{im}, or the same level of math ability, should get the same exact score on y_{ij}. Their score is entirely dependent on the latent variable and nothing else. The challenge, of course, is that we never know someone's value of η_{im}, because it is latent – we must infer whether measurement bias is present using a few modifications of the latent variable models shown above.

The condition shown in Equation 9 is described as *full invariance* (Millsap, 2011). Though it describes the ideal situation, in reality it is difficult to achieve – it is generally improbable that there will be absolutely no differences on the basis of some extraneous covariates on any of a test's items. It is also very difficult to test this condition mathematically. Usually, we are testing a somewhat weaker condition, which is referred to as *first-order invariance* (Millsap, 2011). The equation corresponding to first-order invariance is as follows:

$$E\left(y_{ij}|\eta_{im},x_i\right) = E\left(y_{ij}|\eta_{im}\right). \tag{10}$$

What this means is that the *expected value* of y_{ij}, conditional on the latent variable η_{im}, does not depend on the covariate x_i. The formulation in Equation 10 is subtly but powerfully different from the one offered earlier. Put another way, it means: even if we cannot guarantee that everything about y_{ij} is the same across all levels of x_{ip}, we can guarantee that our predictions for values of y_{ij} does not depend on levels of x_{ip}. Using the example above, this formulation essentially means: an item measuring children's math ability is free of bias on the basis of gender if, given information about a child's math ability, knowing their gender would not cause us to make a different prediction about their score on this item. There may be subtle differences in sources of error, which cause actual scores on the item to deviate from predicted scores, but the predicted score would be the same across gender.

In addition to representing a less stringent condition for the data to meet, this formulation of first-order invariance also allows us to define measurement bias mathematically using the terms we have already presented. Note that, in Equations 3–8, the expected value of y_{ij} (there denoted μ_{ij}) is entirely a function of the latent variable η_{im} and the measurement parameters, λ_{jm}, ν_j, and, if thresholds are being modeled, τ_{jk}. Thus, since we are dealing with expected values, looking for measurement bias means looking for differences across values of x_i in these parameters. So we can mathematically define measurement bias as: any differences on the basis of any covariate x_i in the values of the measurement parameters.

We will now formally define the different types of measurement noninvariance in terms of the different parameters they affect, and the corresponding effects they have on the expected values of items. Using this formulation, we are now ready to distinguish between the different types of DIF we can observe. For this, we refer to Figures 1 and 2, in which the relation between η_{im} and y_{ij} are shown based on different values of the parameters introduced in the previous section. Plots such as these are termed *trace line* plots, and they can be useful tools for understanding the differences between groups in measurement.

We are presenting differences in these parameters in the context of a multiple-groups scenario with two groups. The grouping variable will be denoted G, and it will have two levels, Group 0 ($G = 0$) and Group 1 ($G = 1$). Assume that group membership is a known variable (e.g., treatment group vs. control group, or groupings based on self-reported gender and age) rather than an unobserved subgroup. We will refer to the groups in this case as the *reference* group for $G = 0$ and the *focal* group for $G = 1$. This terminology stems from the case in which there is one group with known measurement parameters (the reference group: $G = 0$), and one in which measurement bias is a concern (the focal group; $G = 1$): but we can apply it to any two-group case. After this section we will describe the actual model formulation for measurement models which allow DIF. As will be shown, we can model DIF on the basis of many different types of variables, not just grouping variables. However, because it is easier to present differences in terms of a simple comparison, we will first present the types of DIF in the two-group case, without loss of generality.

3.1 Differences in the Overall Level of the Item: v_j

As noted earlier, the intercept parameter v_j denotes the intercept for item j. This parameter represents the predicted value of the item for a subject with a value of 0 for all of the latent variables. If there is measurement bias in this parameter for grouping variable g, this means that one of the groups gives higher or lower predicted values of the items than the other, controlling for the latent variable.

The interpretation of this parameter depends on the type of item y_{ij}. If y_{ij} is a continuous item, then the intercept represents the actual value we predict someone with $\eta_{im} = 0$ for all η_{im} to endorse. So if members of Group 1 have a higher value of v_j than members of Group 0, then members of Group 1 are

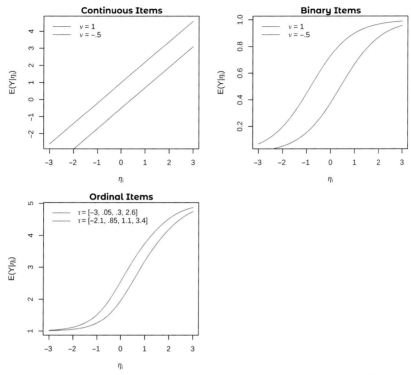

Figure 1 Examples of uniform DIF in continuous, binary, and ordinal items
Note. Figures plot the expected value of y_{ij} against the latent variable η_i. Note the different intercept values for continuous and binary items, and different threshold values for ordinal items, in the upper left-hand corner of the graphs.

predicted to give higher overall responses to y_{ij}, even if they have the same value of the latent variable η_{im}. For instance, suppose that we are measuring a single latent variable, responsive parenting, and y_{ij} is the amount of time a parent spends playing with their child during a free-play task. Further suppose that parents in Group 1 (which could be any grouping variable – older parents relative to younger ones, male parents relative to non-male ones, parents in a treatment condition relative to the control group) have higher values of v_j than those in Group 0. In this case, if we took two parents who had the exact same level of responsiveness, but one parent was from Group 1 and the other was from Group 0, we would predict that the parent from Group 1 plays with their child more than the one from Group 0, even though in reality they are equally responsive. One possible relation between the item and the latent variable is shown in the top left portion of Figure 1. Notice that the lines are parallel: it is only their intercept, representing their overall level of responsiveness, that has changed.

If y_{ij} is binary or ordinal, the interpretation of v_j changes. If y_{ij} is binary, v_j represents the probability of endorsing the item. Suppose we are still measuring responsive parenting, but the item y_{ij} in this case is a binary response variable of whether the parent endorses the item: "I try to take my child's moods into account when interacting with them." In this case, if members of Group 1 had a higher value of v_j than those in Group 0, then we would predict that a parent from Group 1 who has the same level of responsiveness as another parent in Group 0, would nevertheless be more likely to endorse this item than their counterpart in Group 0. The interpretation is only slightly different for ordinal items. If the item were instead a five-level ordinal one, a higher value of v_j in Group 1 would be interpreted as a higher probability of endorsing any category k, relative to category $k-1$ (i.e., the next category down). In this case, we would predict that a parent in Group 1 is more likely than a parent in Group 0 to endorse a higher category, even at the same level of responsiveness. Note that this difference is the exact same across all categories – that is, if Group 1 has a higher value of v_j, then they are more likely to endorse category 4 relative to category 3, category 3 versus 2, category 2 versus 1, and category 1 versus 0. A possible relation between the item and the latent variable is shown in Figure 1, both for the binary and the ordinal cases. Note that, just as in the case of continuous variables, the difference between the trace lines is best described as a horizontal shift, whereby one trace line is associated with higher values of $E(y_{ij}|\eta)$ than the other at every value of η_{ij}. That is, while the expected value of y_{ij} may change, it does so uniformly.

3.2 Differences in the Relation Between the Latent Variable and the Item: λ_{jm}

If v_j can be considered as the intercept for a given item, the loading λ_{jm} represents the regression coefficient that conveys the effect of the latent variable η_m on this item. Thus, if there are differences on the basis of grouping variable g in λ_{jm}, that means that there are differences in the nature of the relation between the latent variable and the items. As with v_j, the interpretation of between-group differences in λ_{jm} differs based on the scale of the item. However, in both cases it can be interpreted as a regression coefficient, with η_{im} as the predictor and y_{ij} as the outcome. The type of regression coefficient is simply a matter of which type of item we are using – if y_{ij} is continuous, λ_{jm} is essentially a linear regression coefficient, but if y_{ij} is binary, λ_{jm} will be a logistic regression coefficient, and so on.

One possible set of relations between η_{im} and y_{ij} with different values of λ_{mj} is shown in Figure 2. Notice a critical difference between the lines shown

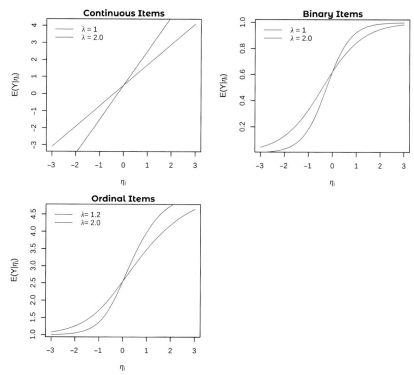

Figure 2 Examples of nonuniform DIF in continuous, binary, and ordinal items

Note. Figures plot the expected value of y_{ij} against the latent variable η_i. Note the different loading values for all items in the upper left-hand corners of the graph.

here and those shown for between-group differences in ν_j: here the lines are not parallel, both for continuous and binary values of y_{ij}. The relation between η_{im} and y_{ij} is stronger in one group than another. Notice that this is the case for all types of items (i.e., continuous, binary, and ordinal). In one group, the predicted value of y_{ij} increases more quickly with corresponding increases in η_{im} than the other group – that is, the relation between η_{im} and y_{ij} is stronger in this group.

Consider our responsive parenting example from earlier. Suppose that item y_{ij} here is the parent's recall of the number of times they drove their children to school. (Note that, this being a count variable, it would likely be better modeled using a Poisson or negative binomial regression than the linear regression we are proposing here. This example is just an illustration; we will treat it as normally distributed for the purpose of argument.) Further suppose that g is a grouping variable based on whether the family lived in an urban, suburban, or rural location. In this case, the number of times the parent drove their child to school may not be a particularly good measure of responsiveness, as it would likely show a weaker relation to responsiveness among urban parents. Parents in urban locations may be very responsive but just not have occasion to drive their children to school, opting instead to accompany them on public transit or walk them to school. In this case, the slope linking η_{im} to y_{ij}, λ_{jm}, would be smaller among urban parents than rural or suburban ones, indicating that as responsiveness increased we would not expect a corresponding increase in y_{ij}. Similarly, if y_{ij} were a binary item asking a parent to recall the last time they drove their child to school, taking a value of 0 if the occasion was over a week ago and a value of 1 if it was within the past week, λ_{jm} would also be smaller. In this case, it would simply mean that, relative to rural or suburban parents, urban parents' probability of driving their children to school does not increase with corresponding increases in responsiveness.

3.3 Differences in the Probability of Endorsing Specific Levels of each Item: τ_{kj}

In an item with multiple possible categories a participant could endorse, recall that there are category-specific threshold parameters, denoted τ_{kjm} for category k of item j measuring latent variable m. A difference between groups may mean many different things, depending on the nature of the item and the differences found therein. In general, such differences occur only if one group is more or less likely to endorse a specific category than the other group, over and above differences in the latent variable.

For instance, suppose we have a four-level ordinal item, and one group has a lower threshold for $k = 4$. What this means is that members of this group are more likely to endorse category 4 than the other group. A between-groups difference such as this one may happen, for instance, if category 4 refers to an event which is extremely common in one group due to factors which are unrelated to the latent variable. Suppose that in our responsive parenting example we had a four-level ordinal item which asked the parent how frequently in the past week they had helped their child get dressed, with response options including *never* (1), *occasionally* (2), *often* (3), and *always* (4). If we created a grouping variable on the basis of the child's age, putting children under three years in the younger group and children over three years in the older group, we might predict that parents with children in the younger group are more likely to endorse the "always" option than those with children in the younger group. Though many children under three years can do some dressing-related tasks, the majority are not able to complete all of the tasks involved in dressing themselves. Perhaps parents of children in the older group would have more latitude to interpret the question – interpreting it, for instance, as the frequency with which they engaged in age-normative tasks relating to dressing oneself such as helping to pick out a matching outfit or helping the child to tie their shoes. But the parents of children in the younger group would be much more likely to say "always."

As one might intuit from the very specific nature of this example that differences in individual thresholds are often difficult to hypothesize a priori. As will be seen shortly, they can also be computationally challenging to model, which leads to some methodological researchers recommending that such differences be modeled sparingly (Gottfredson et al., 2019).

3.4 Differences That Do Not Represent Measurement Bias

We have stated that measurement bias is present if there are differences between groups in the measurement parameters. However, there is another reason that we may observe differences between groups in the latent variables: it may be the case that there actually are differences in the latent variable. In particular, the latent variable mean α_m, as well as latent variable variances ψ_m^2 and covariances ψ_{lm} may differ between groups. We will use the term *impact* to describe such differences.

Differences between groups in α_m, which we will refer to as *mean impact*, are some of the between-group differences in which researchers are often most interested. Consider our responsive parenting example. In this case, we may be interested in whether one group is actually more responsive on average than the other group. For instance, there is evidence that chaotic home environments (i.e., environments lacking in routine and structure) are conducive to less responsive parenting (Vernon-Feagans et al., 2016; Wachs et al., 2013). If we separated our sample into groups according to household chaos level, we may well find that the mean of responsive parenting was higher among parents who reported living in less chaotic homes, relative to their high-chaos counterparts. Similarly, if we were conducting an intervention trial and measuring postintervention levels of responsiveness, perhaps we would find mean differences on the basis of condition, with those in the treatment condition showing higher means than those in the control condition.

Differences between groups in the variance components, which we refer to as *variance impact*, is also common. It may be the case, for instance, that certain groups of parents show more variability in their responsiveness than others. For instance, it may be the case that, in addition to being more responsive overall, parents in less-chaotic homes are more uniformly responsive than those in highly chaotic homes. That is, though we do not have evidence to cite here as in the case of latent variable means, we might speculate that parents living in highly predictable environments are generally all highly responsive, which would mean that the variance of responsiveness in that group would be low since all parents show the same high level of responsiveness. By contrast, parents living in chaotic environments could be more variable in their overall level of responsiveness.

We will now map the above-mentioned differences in the parameters, as defined in this section, onto terminologies and conventions from the SEM and IRT traditions of latent variable modeling.

4 Codifying Measurement Noninvariance and Differential Item Functioning in Different Latent Variable Frameworks

Though measurement invariance and DIF refer to the same fundamental concept, SEM and IRT have different ways of thinking about it. As noted earlier, questions of measurement invariance are typically explored in the SEM framework, particularly within the common factor model; by contrast, the study of DIF has arisen largely from the IRT literature. Critically, field-specific distinctions have faded in recent decades, with both fields' methods generally being united under the heading of nonlinear factor analysis (Wirth & Edwards, 2007). However, the historical differences between the fields matter, because the procedures, goals, and types of items associated with these two modeling traditions have given rise to a number of differences which the reader is likely to hear as they study measurement-related questions. So we will make a few generalizations about the differences between the two fields, recognizing that they are oversimplified, in the interest of providing a broad summary of a complicated distinction.

The broadest distinction comes down to differences in the patterns of measurement bias that are interpreted, as well as what these patterns are called. We explore these patterns now.

4.1 Types of Invariance in SEM

In general, within SEM the question of invariance is considered at the level of the test, with increasingly stringent invariance conditions which must be met for the results to be interpreted (Meredith, 1993). These levels are shown in Figure 3. There are a few things to note about the depiction of invariance in Figure 3, some of which reflect broader points about measurement invariance in SEM. First, we are considering a two-group case. The path diagram on the left is for our first group (here denoted Group 0) and the path diagram on the right is our second group (here denoted Group 1). We will discuss multiple-group analysis shortly ("Multiple-groups formulation"). In the meantime, note that the depiction here includes two types of parameters: intercepts v_{jg} and loadings λ_{jmg}. This g subscript, which is simply the last number in the subscript of parameters that are allowed to vary across groups, represents group membership. Second, notice that there are no threshold parameters τ_{ikj} here. In general, the original formulation of measurement invariance within an SEM context focuses more on differences in items' overall levels (i.e., intercepts) and relations to the latent variable (i.e., loadings). Thus, testing for DIF in individual thresholds does not correspond to any of the types of invariance we will name in this section. We will see shortly, however, that it certainly possible to model differences in thresholds at this stage.

The most fundamental form of invariance, shown in the top panel, is configural invariance, which holds if the same factors account for the same items across groups (Horn & McArdle, 1992). The assumption of configural invariance would be violated if, for instance, there are three factors in one group and two factors in the other. In general, absent configural invariance no inferences can be drawn about differences between groups. Having established configural invariance, we then examine metric, scalar, and strict measurement invariance (Steenkamp & Baumgartner, 1998; Vandenberg & Lance, 2000). Note that metric invariance is sometimes referred to as "weak metric invariance," and scalar invariance is sometimes referred to as "strong metric invariance."

The first two of these conditions are shown in Figure 3. Under metric invariance, the factor loadings Λ must be equal across all values of G. That is, we assume that the strength of the relations between the latent variable and the outcomes are the same across groups. Under scalar invariance, metric invariance must hold and, additionally, measurement intercepts v must be equal across all values of G. In other words, scalar invariance means that the overall level of the items, over and above the latent variable itself, is the same across groups – members of one group are no more or less likely to endorse the items than the other.

Finally, under strict measurement invariance, both metric and scalar measurement invariance must hold, but the error covariance matrix Σ must also be equal across all values of G. Note that strict invariance, thus, is required to fulfill the definition of full invariance offered above in Equation 9. The ramifications of violations of these assumptions are discussed below.

The concept of *partial invariance* was introduced into the CFA tradition to refer to the case in which some, but not all, measurement parameters are invariant (Byrne et al., 1989; Cheung & Rensvold, 2002a). In such a case, for instance, two loadings could be noninvariant, along with three intercepts. The

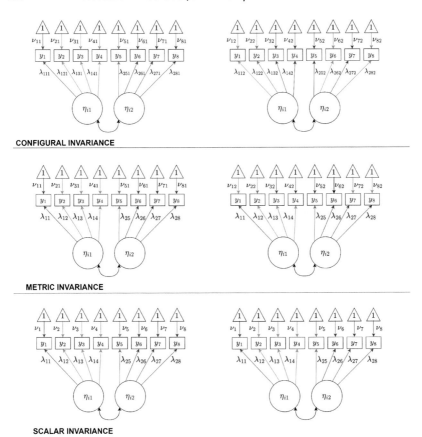

Figure 3 Different types of measurement invariance under the SEM framework

Note. Path diagrams for two-group latent variable models under configural invariance (top), metric invariance (middle), and scalar invariance (bottom). The 1's in triangles are standard notation for intercepts; the path between the 1 and the indicator, given by v_{jg}, represents the intercept. Different colored arrows indicate differences across the two groups. Note that both loadings and intercepts differ in configural invariance; only intercepts differ in metric invariance; and neither loadings nor intercepts differ for scalar invariance.

case of partial invariance leads to an important question: How much invariance is "enough" for the groups to be truly comparable in terms of the latent variable? Broadly, there is no one right answer to this question. For one thing, there are many ways in which to measure the overall amount of DIF on an item or a set of items. With respect to partial invariance, however, there are many ways to even consider the question of how much DIF is too much. Should we consider it in terms of the number of items with DIF, the number of unique effects, the magnitude of each DIF effect, or some other way? Though these questions do not have a single answer, some evidence can be drawn from empirical studies of the consequences of DIF. We discuss these studies in the section "Empirical findings: Does DIF actually matter?".

4.2 Types of DIF in IRT

By contrast to SEM, in IRT DIF is typically explored at the level of individual items. That is, whereas SEM starts from the question of whether all items are invariant and proceeds to test partial invariance only after that omnibus condition has been tested, IRT starts from the question of whether each individual item is invariant (Mellenbergh, 1989). Consequently, within IRT DIF is typically tested at the level of each item. *Uniform DIF* refers to differences in the predicted value of y_{ij} that are the same across all levels of the latent variable. In binary or continuous items, this typically corresponds to differences in the v_j parameter. Recall that, as we noted earlier, the trace lines of two groups who differ in v_j do not cross – predicted values are simply higher for one group than another. By contrast, *nonuniform DIF* refers to differences in the predicted values of y_{ij} that differ across levels of the latent variable. Nonuniform DIF typically corresponds to differences across groups in λ_{im}, indicating a differential relation between the latent variable and the outcome. Note that, as before, this essentially refers to an interaction – as the latent variable's value changes, differences across groups may be exacerbated or attenuated. Each of these trace lines are depicted with respect to binary and continuous items in Figures 1 and 2, as discussed earlier.

There are a few issues of which readers will want to take note with this terminology. First, though uniform and nonuniform DIF are terms which are typically applied to differences in intercepts v_j and loadings λ_{mj} respectively, the broadest definition of nonuniform DIF also includes differences across groups in τ_{jk}. That is, because the predicted value of the item may change across groups to a different extent at different values of η_{im}, this type of DIF is still nonuniform. Another issue with this terminology is that some authors use the terms *uniform* and *nonuniform* to refer to differences in the direction of DIF effects across items within a given test (Chen, 2007; Yoon & Millsap, 2007). That is, if a test has two items with DIF on v_j and both are in the same direction (i.e., the differences both favor the same group), that is referred to as uniform DIF. By contrast, if the DIF on v_j is nonuniform, it may be the case that the difference on one item has a higher value of v_j in one group, and the other has a higher value of v_h in the other group, $h \neq j$. We will not use this terminology here, but readers should know that it is present.

4.3 A Further Note about Similarities and Differences Between SEM- and IRT-Based Methods

Though the terms used by SEM and IRT to describe DIF are different, it is also important to note that they are in many ways the same. Uniform DIF maps relatively well onto a lack of scalar measurement invariance – that is, a uniform difference across groups in the average predicted value of y_{ij}. By contrast, nonuniform DIF maps onto the idea of metric invariance; it represents a difference across groups in the predicted increment in y_{ij} associated with a one-unit shift in η_{im}. The main difference between the frameworks, as we have reviewed them so far, is in the unit of analysis. Whereas SEM generally treats the whole set of items as potentially noninvariant in terms of all items' overall endorsement levels and relations to the latent variable (scalar and metric noninvariance, respectively), IRT most often considers whether individual items themselves vary across groups in terms of their overall endorsement levels and relationsips to the latent variable (uniform and nonuniform DIF, respectively). Nevertheless, despite the similarities between them, SEM and IRT have historically been motivated by different considerations, and procedures for testing for measurement noninvariance/DIF vary accordingly.

An important set of distinctions arises from the types of items which SEM and IRT typically consider, as well as the nature of the latent variables they are assumed to measure. Historically, the modal use of IRT has been to measure a single latent variable with a relatively large number (e.g., >8) of items, which are often binary or ordinal. There are many exceptions to this, with a number of IRT models for more than one latent variable, as well as contexts in which items are continuous (e.g., Ferrando, 2002; Reckase, 1997). By contrast, SEM is typically applied when it is presumed that there are multiple latent variables, with the nature of these variables and the relations among them being of primary interest. Additionally, SEM has historically applied the assumption of multivariate normality to items, making it well suited to cases in which items are truly continuous.

The first reason this matters is that, with items of different scales, different sorts of invariance are possible, Notice that, though invariance of parameters v_j (codified at the single-item level as uniform DIF on v_j in IRT, at the test level as scalar invariance in v in CFA) and λ_{jm} (nonuniform DIF on λ_{jm} in IRT, metric invariance in Λ in CFA) are described by both frameworks, equivalence of error terms is described only in CFA, as strict invariance. In CFA with continuous items, strict invariance is required to fulfill the definition of full invariance shown in Equation 9. In IRT with dichotomous variables, first-order invariance is equivalent to the full definition of measurement invariance from Equation 9;

this is because a conditional variance of y_{ij} is not defined. Given polytomous variables, first-order invariance and full invariance may differ, but under most commonly used IRT models they are the same (Chang & Mazzeo, 1994).

The second reason it matters is that, as we will see, the types of models and testing procedures used to find measurement noninvariance/DIF are informed by the types of items and latent variables being considered. Though there are many exceptions to this distinction, in general procedures arising from the CFA tradition focus on establishing the structure of factors across groups, whereas those arising from IRT focus on finding the optimal set of items to measure a construct (Stark et al., 2004, 2006; Wirth & Edwards, 2007). We discuss this broadly in the section "Consequences of Measurement Noninvariance and Differential Item Functioning" and specifically when reviewing procedures for locating DIF ("Detecting Measurement Noninvariance and Differential Item Functioning").

5 Models for Measurement Noninvariance and Differential Item Functioning

If we are thinking of measurement bias in terms of differences between individuals in parameter values, the next question becomes: How do we model such differences in parameters? There are extensions of both SEM and IRT which allow for parameters to differ across a grouping variable – i.e., multiple-groups SEM (Jöreskog, 1971) and multiple-groups IRT (Bock & Zimowski, 1997). It is in the context of multiple-groups models that many tests for measurement bias have been developed. In recent decades a new set of models, which allow differences in parameters to be modeled according to a wider range of variables, have entered the fray, including multiple-indicator/multiple-cause (MIMIC; Finch, 2005; Muthén, 1989) and moderated nonlinear factor analysis (MNLFA) models (Bauer, 2017; Bauer & Hussong, 2009); we refer to these as "regression-based" formulations. We introduce DIF first in the context of a multiple-groups formulation, and end with the regression-based formulation. We will demonstrate these in the context of a worked example, which we introduce briefly first.

5.1 Data Example: Longitudinal Study of Australian Children

From this point on, we will be demonstrating each model we discuss using real data arising from the Longitudinal Study of Australian Children (LSAC; Sanson et al., 2002). Data access must be requested from the Australian Institute of Family Studies, but all study scripts are available in the Supplemental Materials

Table 3 Items in the parental warmth scale

Item	Question
Item 1	How often do you express affection by hugging, kissing, and holding this child?
Item 2	How often do you hug or hold this child for no particular reason?
Item 3	How often do you tell this child how happy he/she makes you?
Item 4	How often do you have warm, close times together with this child?
Item 5	How often do you enjoy doing things with this child?
Item 6	How often do you feel close to this child both when he/she is happy and when he/she is upset?

of this report, as well as this Git repository: `https://github.com/vtcole/element`.

Though the data are described completely elsewhere (Gray & Sanson, 2005; Zubrick et al., 2014), we summarize the dataset briefly here. The data ($N = 4,359$; 51% male) come from a nationally representative longitudinal study of children in Australia, whose parents participated in the first wave of the study in 2004. In two-parent households, both parents answered the survey when possible; for each participant, one parent was sampled randomly. There are two cohorts of LSAC, one which started shortly after the child was born and one which started when the child was in kindergarten; we use exclusively the birth cohort here. Data come from the first wave of assessment, when most children were in their first year of life ($M_{age} = 39.90$ weeks; range $= 14$–103 weeks). Note that the study used complex sampling, and we will use sampling weights in our analyses for demonstration purposes. However, when using only a subset of the sample that has been sampled in this way (as we are here), there are generally a few more data management steps to take; we forego these here as they are not the focus on the current demonstration.

For this analysis, we are interested in parental warmth, which was measured using the six items shown in Table 3 (Cohen et al., 1977). Responses were on a five-point scale, with response options of *never/almost never* (1), *rarely* (2), *sometimes* (3), *often* (4), and *always/almost always* (5). Internal consistency for this scale was strong, with $\alpha = 0.838$. We will examine the effects of three covariates: child sex (male vs. female), parent gender (male vs. female), and child age in weeks. Note that we use child sex and parent gender, because parents reported their gender identity but we only have information about biological sex for children. We consider age in two ways: as a grouping variable with four levels corresponding to the four quartiles of age, and as a continuous variable in its original metric (i.e., weeks).

The bulk of this section will introduce two main formulations of models which can be used to answer questions about noninvariance and DIF. Importantly, the purpose of these models is twofold. First, they can be used to assess whether noninvariance or DIF are present. Second, given that noninvariance or DIF are found, they can be used to model those effects, with the goal of eliminating their biasing effects on estimates of the latent variable parameters. However, just as in any analysis, we must conduct a series of exploratory steps before proceeding with the modeling process. We discuss these now.

5.2 A Preliminary Step: Data Visualization and Data Management

As in just about any modeling context, it is critical in the study of measurement invariance to visualize the data before conducting any analyses. We conducted a series of data visualization and management steps with the example data in R, which are given in the Supplemental Materials.

There are two goals of data visualization. The first is to determine which items require further data management before proceeding. In particular, it is critical to make sure that y_{ij} has enough variation, ideally both in the aggregate and at specific levels of the covariate, for us to model. For ordinal items, this means determining whether the endorsement rates of each level are sufficient to keep all levels, or whether we must collapse sparsely endorsed item categories. This decision does entail some loss of information. However, in many cases collapsing across sparsely endorsed categories yields more stable results and greater convergence rates, relative to retaining a level of the item which few subjects endorse (DiStefano et al., 2021).

In the example data, we find the endorsement rates shown in Figure 4. We notice that for all items except Item 3, the lower two categories (rarely and sometimes) were seldom endorsed. Thus, we collapse all items except Item 3 to a three-level variable, retaining all five levels for Item 3.

The second reason to visualize the data is that it may give us some clues about what to expect in our analyses, and give us a sense of what those results will mean in practical terms. Though there are many analyses which may be useful (in addition to the checks for sufficient variance described above), we suggest two. The first is to plot the means (or endorsement probabilities) of each item by levels of the covariates. This step helps us to see whether one or more items does not appear to show the same general behavior as others.

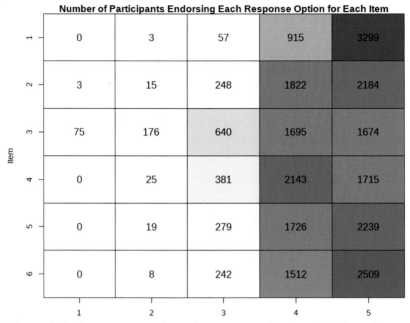

Figure 4 Endorsement rates for each response option for all six items in our data example from the Longitudinal Study of Australian Children (LSAC; $N = 4,359$)

Note. The number in each cell represents the number of participants who endorsed the corresponding response option for the corresponding item.

We have done this for the example data in Figure 5. Note that, to get all the item means onto comparable scales, we centered each item's mean so that the middle response option is zero. There are a few differences between groups, most noticeably that male parents show lower means of all items than female parents. However, here we are looking for items which deviate from the pattern shown by all others. The only potentially suspicious items are Item 3 and, to a lesser extent, Item 5, which appear to be higher among parents of younger children, by contrast to most of the others, which are lower. These may be items on which we can expect to see DIF.

We also recommend looking at correlation matrices by levels of each covariate. This step helps to give a sense of whether some relations are weaker or stronger at certain levels of the covariate, which may Lewis as nonuniform DIF later on. We have depicted the correlation matrices in the example data according to each level of age quartile in Figure 6. Corresponding plots for different levels of child sex and parent gender can be obtained using the code in the Supplemental Materials. (Note that researchers do not have to depict each correlation coefficient graphically – merely examining the matrix may

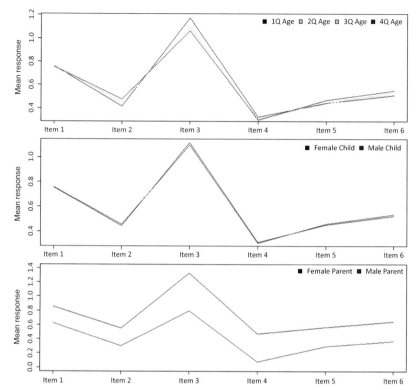

Figure 5 Mean item responses at each level of child age, child sex, and parent gender in our data example from the Longitudinal Study of Australian Children (LSAC; $N = 4,359$)
Note. The number in each cell represents the number of participants who endorsed the corresponding response option for the corresponding item.

be sufficient.) We do not see anything too troubling with the example data, although there may be subtle DIF effects that do not manifest here.

We are now ready to fit our models to the example data. We articulate the two broad classes of models – multiple-groups and regression-based models – and demonstrate them in the context of this example.

5.3 Multiple-groups Formulation

Multiple-groups models are particularly useful in that they allow the same model –in our case, the model outlined in Equations 2–8 – to be fit in multiple different groups, with parameters that may differ across the groups (Jöreskog, 1971). If we use the same formulation as before, we have measured J items ($j = 1, \ldots, J$) for N participants ($i = 1, \ldots, N$); each item for each participant is denoted y_{ij}. These items measure M latent variables ($m = 1, \ldots, M$); each

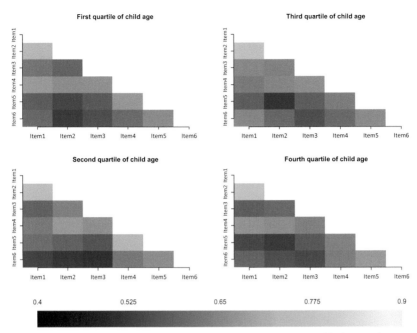

Figure 6 Polychoric correlation matrix for each age quartile in our data example from the Longitudinal Study of Australian Children (LSAC; $N = 4,359$)

Note. Correlations ranged from $r = 0.4$ to $r = 0.9$. The relation between color and correlation coefficients is shown in the bottom of the figure.

participant's value of the latent variable is denoted η_{im}. If we extend this to a multiple-groups case, we assume that the participants fall into one of N_G groups $(g = 1, \ldots, N_G)$.

The multiple groups nonlinear factor model allows us to model N_G sets of parameters. That is, there could be N_G sets of measurement parameters for each group; the parameters for group g are subscripted with g, so that we have item intercepts ν_{jg}, λ_{jmg}, τ_{jkg}, and so on. Similarly, the latent variable means, variances, and covariances can vary across groups, with the parameters for group g including mean α_{mg}, variance ψ_{mg}^2, and latent variable covariances $\psi_{mqg}, q \neq m$. Taken together, this means that the groups may potentially differ in terms of both the latent variables and the measurement parameters; in other words, they could have completely different relations between the latent variable and the items. The caveat, of course, is that the model must be identified, which precludes all of the item parameters varying across groups. Typically at least one item's parameters must be the same across groups, and potentially further constrained (e.g., its factor loading set to 1 and its intercept set to 0). However, there are a number of ways to identify the model, as described in greater detail below.

In the multiple-groups context, we would say that there is first-order measurement invariance across the N_G groups if values of the measurement parameters λ_{jmg}, ν_{jg}, and τ_{jkg} (if estimated) are equal for all values of g. In other words, measurement invariance is codified as the lack of differences in the values of measurement parameters between groups. Similarly, we can test for differences across groups in the mean α_{mg}, variance ψ_{mg}^2, and latent variable covariances $\psi_{mqg}, q \neq m$. These are often the parameter differences that correspond to a researcher's substantive questions – for example, are there differences in depressive symptoms between subjects of different genders? Are the relation between internalizing and externalizing psychopathology the same across age groups? – and distinguishing these differences from measurement bias is one of the key tasks of measurement invariance analysis.

How exactly do we test whether there are differences across groups? We can use a *likelihood ratio test*, which assesses whether the fit of one model, which we denote the constrained model, is inferior to that of a more complicated model, which we denote the full model. The log-likelihoods are obtained and a test statistic, equal to -2 times the difference in the log-likelihoods, is computed; this test statistic is roughly χ^2 distributed with *df* equal to the difference between the models in the number of parameters.

The logic of likelihood ratio tests within multiple-groups models is explained fully elsewhere (Satorra & Saris, 1985). However, the basic premise is that a model with no differences between groups in parameters is a simpler version of the model which allows these differences. For example, suppose we have two groups, and we are interested in whether the factor loading of the jth item for the mth latent variable is invariant across the groups. If we set all values of $\lambda_{jm0} = \lambda_{jm1}$ for groups 0 and 1, we are estimating fewer parameters than a model in which these parameters are allowed to differ across the two groups. So the model with measurement invariance in λ_{jmg} is our constrained model; the model without measurement invariance, which allows λ_{jmg} to differ across groups, is our full model.

There are a number of points of which researchers should be aware when using likelihood ratio tests. First, it is necessary to note that when certain estimators are used (e.g., maximum likelihood estimation for categorical or non-normal continuous response variables, which we use here), a correction factor is applied to the loglikelihoods. Thus, rather than a "standard" likelihood ratio test, we must incorporate these correction factors into the likelihood ratio test statistic (Satorra & Bentler, 2001). If we denote the loglikelihoods of the more restricted and less restricted models LL_0 and LL_1, respectively; the number of parameters in each as p_0 and p_1, respectively; and the correction factor for each as c_0 and c_1, respectively; we compute the likelihood ratio test statistic as:

$$LRT = \frac{-2\,(LL_1 - LL_0)}{cd}, \tag{11}$$

where

$$cd = \frac{p_0 c_0 - p_1 c_1}{p_0 - p_1}. \tag{12}$$

Note that this correction applies to any loglikelihood calculated using robust maximum likelihood, which we use as a default when estimating nonlinear factor models. Thus, it is our standard approach.

The second major point is a caveat about the potential usefulness of likelihood ratio tests. It has been noted that likelihood ratio tests depend on sample size, with so much statistical power at large sample sizes that even trivial differences between models may be significant (Brannick, 1995). To get around this issue, some have proposed comparing fit indices commonly used in SEM, between more and less constrained models (Cheung & Rensvold, 2002a). Among others, this includes the comparative fit index (CFI; Bentler, 1990), Tucker–Lewis Index (TLI; Tucker & Lewis, 1973) and the root mean squared error of approximation (RMSEA; Steiger, 1998). A researcher might, for instance, note that the CFI values (which takes values between 0 and 1, with values closer to 1 indicating better model fit) are 0.95 and 0.98 for a scalar and metric invariance model, respectively, and favor the model with metric invariance because it improves the CFI substantially. Results from a number of simulation studies have indicated that differences in these fit indices are in many cases more sensitive to noninvariance than likelihood ratio tests (Meade et al., 2008).

The final major point to note is that likelihood ratio tests (and the fit statistics based on them) are not appropriate for all model testing situations. In particular, the χ^2 distribution of likelihood ratio test statistics depends on the less restrictive model being correctly specified (Maydeu-Olivares & Cai, 2006; Yuan & Bentler, 2004). As such, if neither of the models being compared is the true model, a likelihood ratio test is not suitable for making measurement invariance comparisons (Schneider et al., 2020). Another distributional assumption of likelihood ratio tests is that the more restricted model is not on the boundary of the parameter space of the less restricted model. Though a more complete discussion of this phenomenon is available elsewhere (Savalei & Kolenikov, 2008; Stoel et al., 2006), one example arises when a researcher is testing whether a variance component is nonzero by comparing a model with the latent variable's variance set to zero (the restricted model) to one in which this variance is freely estimated. Because all variances must be equal to or greater than zero, the restricted model has fixed the variance to the "boundary" of permissible values such a parameter can take. A more complete and technical presentation of this issue is available at the above-noted references, but researchers should at least be aware that there are some models which cannot be compared (Savalei & Kolenikov, 2008; Stoel et al., 2006).

5.3.1 Data Example

We tested the levels of invariance shown in Figure 3 in our example data. Mplus code for fitting all models is available in the Supplemental Materials.

Conducting these tests involved expanding a bit on the series of models shown in Figure 3. First, the classification of measurement invariance shown in Figure 3 does not explicitly refer to measurement invariance in individual thresholds for different categories (τ_{kjg}) when using ordinal data. Thus, for models in which intercepts are allowed to vary (i.e., configural and metric invariance) we tested two versions: one in which differences in intercepts were tested, and one in which differences in individual thresholds were tested. We tested models for three grouping variables: child sex (0 = female; 1 = male), parent gender (0 = female; 1 = male), and child age quartile (0 = first quartile; 1 = second quartile; 2 = third quartile; 4 = fourth quartile). Thus, for each of these grouping variables we tested a multiple-group version of the models outlined in Equations 6–8, with the following set of constraints:

1. **Configural with thresholds**: A model with configural invariance, in which loadings (λ_{mjg}) and individual thresholds (τ_{kjg}) are allowed to vary across groups; the intercept parameter (v_{jg}) is constrained to zero in all groups.
2. **Configural with intercepts**: A model with configural invariance, in which loadings (λ_{mjg}) and intercepts (v_{jg}) are allowed to vary across groups but individual thresholds are not.
3. **Metric with thresholds**: A model with metric invariance, in which loadings (λ_{mjg}) are constrained to equality across all groups but individual thresholds (τ_{kjg}) are allowed to vary across groups; the intercept parameter (v_{jg}) is set to zero in all groups.
4. **Metric with intercepts**: A model with metric invariance, in which loadings (λ_{mjg}) are constrained to equality across all groups but intercepts (v_{jg}) are allowed to vary across groups.
5. **Scalar**: A model with scalar invariance, in which loadings (λ_{mjg}), intercepts (v_{jg}), and thresholds (τ_{kjg}) are constrained to equality across groups.

Model identification is discussed formally below ("Model identification and anchor items"). However, we note here that each set of models imposed a number of constraints for identification purposes. First, each model in which loadings and/or intercepts were allowed to vary across classes, we used Item 1 as our anchor item. We chose Item 1 on the basis of it appearing to behave similarly across groups in the data visualization step (described in the previous section). However, the importance of anchor items is discussed at greater length below, both by way of a formal definition ("Model identification and anchor items") and an empirical review of the literature on anchor item selection ("Consequences of measurement noninvariance"). Second, we estimated differences across groups in the latent variable by constraining the latent variable's mean α_g and variance ψ_g^2 to 0 and 1, respectively, and freely estimating these parameters in other groups.

We conducted likelihood ratio tests comparing each successive level of invariance to the next. For each grouping variable, this entailed four tests: one comparing Models 1 (configural with thresholds) and 3 (metric with thresholds), one comparing Models 2 (configural with intercepts) and 4 (metric with intercepts), one comparing Models 3 (metric with thresholds) and 5 (scalar), and one comparing Models 4 (metric with intercepts) and 5. Note that, as written, models with differences across groups in intercepts (e.g., Models 2 and 4) are not nested within models with differences across groups in individual thresholds (e.g., Models 1 and 3); thus, we do not compare these models in our tables. However, a model with intercept differences can be re-parameterized to show that it is nested within a model with threshold differences; indeed, this is how we parameterize it in the Mplus code in the Supplemental Material. For simplicity's sake, we do not demonstrate here why this is the case, although it will come up in a few special cases shortly.

Loglikelihoods and model comparisons for each model are shown in Table 4. Note that, due to our use of ordinal response variables with maximum likelihood, we are unable to get the fit indices (e.g., Comparative Fit Index, Tucker–Lewis Index) mentioned earlier. As a reminder, Models 1 and 2 were configural invariance models, allowing between-group differences in loadings and either item thresholds (Model 1) or item intercepts (Model 2); Models 3 and 4 were metric invariance models which constrained Model 1 and 2 respectively by holding loadings equal across groups; and Model 5 was a scalar invariance model which held loadings, intercepts, and thresholds equal across groups.

For child sex, scalar invariance was supported by all model comparisons. In other words, fit was not improved by removing constraints on intercepts (Model 4 vs. Model 5) or thresholds (Model 3 vs. Model 5), nor by removing constraints on factor loadings (Model 1 vs. Model 3; Model 2 vs. Model 4). In other words, we have evidence that Model 5, the simplest model, essentially fits just as well as the more complex models we fit. Thus, Model 5 is the final model; it is shown

Table 4 Model fit and model comparisons for all multiple-groups models testing successive levels of invairance in our data example from the Longitudinal Study of Australian Children (LSAC; $N = 4,359$)

Child sex

	Model fit			Model comparison					
	N_{par}	LL	CF	More restricted model	$\Delta(N_{par})$	χ^2	CF	p	Comparison
Model 1	40	−21627.803	1.140	Model 3	5	5.936	1.191	0.313	Metric vs. configural
Model 2	33	−21629.616	1.143	Model 4	5	4.859	1.151	0.433	Metric vs. configural
Model 3	35	−21631.339	1.133	Model 5	12	3.752	1.080	0.988	Scalar vs. metric
Model 4	28	−21632.437	1.139	Model 5	5	1.782	1.041	0.878	Scalar vs. metric
Model 5	23	−21633.364	1.161						

Parent gender

	N_{par}	LL	CF	More restricted model	$\Delta(N_{par})$	χ^2	CF	p	Comparison
Model 1	40	−21292.550	1.166	Model 3	5	8.492	1.198	0.131	Metric vs. configural
Model 2	33	−21312.932	1.156	Model 4	5	21.914	1.091	<0.001	Metric vs. configural
Model 3	35	−21297.636	1.161	Model 5	12	83.609	1.147	<0.001	Scalar vs. metric
Model 4	28	−21324.891	1.168	Model 5	5	35.499	1.167	<0.001	Scalar vs. metric
Model 5	23	−21345.598	1.168						

Child age

	N_{par}	LL	CF	More restricted model	$\Delta(N_{par})$	χ^2	CF	p	Comparison
Model 1	78	−24544.744	1.155	Model 3	15	18.047	1.203	0.260	Metric vs. configural
Model 2	57	−24555.844	1.135	Model 4	15	22.149	1.114	0.104	Metric vs. configural
Model 3	63	−24555.595	1.144	Model 5	34	52.830	1.107	0.021	Scalar vs. metric
Model 4	44	−24567.457	1.147	Model 5	15	32.501	1.069	0.006	Scalar vs. metric
Model 5	29	−24584.835	1.187						

Note. N_{par} denotes the number of parameters in a given model; LL denotes the loglikelihood; CF denotes the correction factor; $\Delta(N_{par})$ denotes the change in the number of parameters from the more restricted model to the less restricted model.

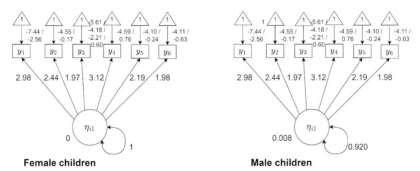

Figure 7 Final multiple-groups model based on child sex in our data example
from the Longitudinal Study of Australian Children (LSAC; $N = 4,359$)
Note. No between-group differences in latent variable means and variances
were significant at the $\alpha = 0.05$ level. Parameter values are given next to the
corresponding arrows for loadings, factor means, and factor variances. Item
thresholds are given next to the triangle for each item; for instance, the
thresholds for endorsing the second and third response options for Item 1 are
-7.44 and -2.58, respectively, in both groups.

in Figure 7. In this model, we freely estimate the mean and variance for boys
but constrain the mean and variance to 0 and 1 for girls to set the scale of the
latent variable. The mean for boys, $\alpha_1 = -.005$, is not significantly different
from zero, from which we infer that there are no differences in the mean level
of parent responsiveness based on child sex.

For parent gender a very different story emerges. Here, scalar invariance is
not supported in any comparison (Model 3 vs. Model 5 or Model 4 vs. Model
5). Moreover, metric invariance is only supported when we allow thresholds to
vary across groups (Model 2 vs. Model 4), not when we only estimate intercept
differences (Model 1 vs. Model 3). That is, the nonsignificant LRT comparing
Model 2 to Model 4 indicates that allowing thresholds to vary across groups
does not improve model fit, whereas the significant LRT comparing Model 1
to Model 3 suggests that allowing intercepts does improve model fit. Taken
together, we take these results as a rejection of metric invariance, albeit an
equivocal one. Thus, either Model 1 or Model 2 should be our final model.
As mentioned earlier, it can be demonstrated that models with between-group
differences in thresholds (i.e., Models 1 and 3) can be reparameterized to be
nested within models with between-group differences in only intercepts (i.e.,
Models 2 and 4). Thus, we tested the fit of Model 1 against Model 2, finding
that Model 1 fit significantly better, $\chi^2(7) = 33.702, p < 0.001$.

Model 1 is, therefore, our final model for parent gender. It is shown in Figure
8. We see that loadings are considerably higher for fathers, relative to mothers,
for a number of items. This difference in loadings suggests that these items

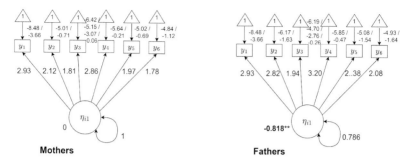

Figure 8 Final multiple-groups model based on parent gender in our data example from the Longitudinal Study of Australian Children (LSAC; $N = 4,359$)

Note. Asterisks denote significant between-group differences in latent variable means. $**p < 0.01$. $*p < 0.05$. $†p < 0.10$. Parameter values are given next to the corresponding arrows for loadings, factor means, and factor variances. Item thresholds are given next to the triangle for each item; for instance, the thresholds for endorsing the second and third response options for Item 1 are -8.48 and -3.66, respectively, in both groups.

are more closely related to parental responsiveness among fathers than among mothers. There is less of a consistent pattern among thresholds, with some items (e.g., Item 2) showing lower thresholds (meaning an overall higher likelihood of endorsement) among fathers, and others (e.g., Item 3) showing lower thresholds among mothers. With respect to the latent variable, we see that the mean for fathers is $alpha_1 = -.818$ and that it is significantly different from zero. We thus conclude that fathers show lower overall levels of responsiveness than mothers.

Finally, with respect to age grouping, we see that metric invariance is supported by both relevant comparisons (Model 1 vs. Model 3, Model 2 vs. Model 4), and scalar invariance is rejected by both relevant comparisons (Model 3 vs. Model 5, Model 4 vs. Model 5). That is, both sets of LRT's informing our conclusions about metric invariance were nonsignificant, and both sets of tests informing our conclusions about scalar invariance were significant. Here too, as with parent gender, we are left to interpret either Model 3 or Model 4 – and here too, we can test a reparameterization of Model 4 against Model 3. When we do so, we find that Model 3 does not provide significant improvement in fit over Model 4, $\chi^2 (19) = 20.8724, p = 0.344$.

Thus, we move forward with Model 4 for age. It is shown in Figure 9. Interestingly, the parameters in Figure 9 give us some insight into the relation between intercept and threshold parameters, as well as why we can reparameterize models with intercept DIF to be nested within those for threshold DIF. Notice that the thresholds differ across age groups, but that they do so uniformly

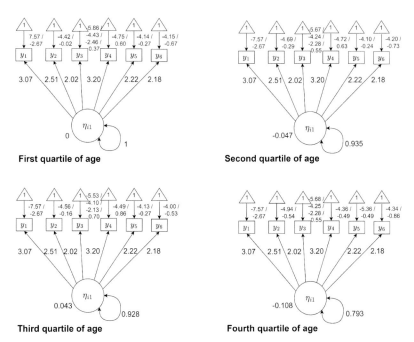

Figure 9 Final multiple-groups model based on child age in our data example from the Longitudinal Study of Australian Children (LSAC; $N = 4,359$) Note. No between-group differences in latent variable means and variances were significant at the $\alpha = 0.05$ level. Parameter values are given next to the corresponding arrows for loadings, factor means, and factor variances. Item thresholds are given next to the triangle for each item; for instance, the thresholds for endorsing the second and third response options for Item 1 are -7.57 and -2.67, respectively, in all groups.

across item categories. For instance, the threshold for choosing the second response option for Item 2 in the youngest quartile, -4.424, is lower than the corresponding threshold in the second-youngest quartile, -4.691. The difference between these groups' thresholds is -4.424 - (-4.691) = 0.267. That is, the threshold for choosing the second response option is 0.267 units higher in the youngest quartile than in the second-youngest quartile. Now notice these groups' thresholds for choosing the first response options: -0.024 in the youngest quartile, and -0.291 in the second-youngest quartile. The difference between these two groups' thresholds is -0.024 - (-0.291) = 0.267. In other words, thresholds for all of the response options for a given item must increase or decrease by the same amount. This formulation is mathematically identical to between-group differences in intercepts.

Looking at the thresholds, we do not see a clear pattern across ages. Thresholds are generally the lowest in the oldest group, but this pattern is not constant across ages (as thresholds are actually the highest in the second-oldest group). We also see no mean differences across age groups – that is, parents do not show more responsive behavior overall across age groups. Findings like these ones are a great example of why interpreting DIF effects substantively is often a bad idea: there is no particular reason why thresholds should vary in this way (i.e., they do not increase or decrease monotonically across ages), and trying to intuit such a reason is often a fool's errand that may lead us to an erroneous conclusion. Thus, in a case like this one we would typically include the DIF effects of age on threshold when generating estimates of factor scores, without interpreting what such effects mean. We elaborate on this reasoning below ("Recommendations for best practices").

5.4 Regression-Based Models

Regression-based models take a different approach to modeling between-group differences in parameters, and just about any multiple-groups model can be reparameterized using a regression-based formulation. However, as will be shown momentarily, their real strength is that they can accommodate types of measurement noninvariance/DIF that multiple-groups models cannot. Rather than testing the null hypothesis that parameter values differ between groups, regression-based formulations model parameters as outcomes in a regression equation with group membership – along with any other person-level variable – as a covariate (Bauer & Hussong, 2009; Finch, 2005).

We start with the formulation of the item response under the nonlinear factor model shown in Equations 2 and 3. As before, λ_{jm} represents the loading linking the mth factor to the jth item, v_j represents the intercept of item j, and, if the data are ordinal, τ_{kj} represents the threshold for the kth category for the jth item. We can alter Equation 2 as follows:

$$\omega_{ij} = v_{ij} + \sum_{m=1}^{M} \lambda_{ijm} \eta_{im}. \tag{13}$$

For ordinal items, we can alter Equation 8 as follows:

$$\omega_{ikj} = \tau_{ikj} - \left(v_{ij} + \sum_{m=1}^{M} \lambda_{ijm} \eta_{im} \right). \tag{14}$$

Note that in both cases the only alteration is the addition of the subscript i to the parameters λ_{ijm}, v_{ij}, and τ_{ikj}. The addition of this subscript may seem minor, but it represents the crucial modification that defines a regression-based approach: each individual i has their own person-specific value of the measurement parameters. Each of the regression parameters is potentially a function of

individual i's value on any number of covariates, which can include potentially
DIF-generating factors such as age, gender, race, and so on.

Two differences from the multiple-groups approach emerge here. Unlike the
multiple-groups approach, these variables may be of any scale; though we could
consider group membership as a covariate, we can also consider continuous or
ordinal variables. Additionally, we can consider each measurement parameter
as a function of multiple covariates at a given time. Note of course that we could
combine covariates to create groupings in the multiple-groups approach – for
instance, in our data example, we could create a grouping variable that sum-
marizes each combination of child sex, parent gender, and child age quartile.
This formulation may be preferable in some cases, such as when we would like
to make comparisons across specific levels of these variables (e.g., comparing
boys in the first quartile of age to girls in the first quartile of age). However,
it would create a large number of groups (in our data example, it would create
$2 \times 2 \times 4 = 16$). One of the approximate methods described below ("Detecting
measurement noninvariance"), alignment, is well suited to this case.

We denote the pth covariate for the ith participant x_{ip}, where P refers to the
number of covariates ($p = 1, \ldots, P$). The regression equation for each of the
measurement parameters in Equations 13 and, if relevant, 14 are as follows:

$$v_{ij} = v_{j0} + \sum_{p=1}^{P} v_{jp} x_{ip}, \tag{15}$$

$$\lambda_{ijm} = \lambda_{jm0} + \sum_{p=1}^{P} \lambda_{jmp} x_{ip}, \tag{16}$$

$$\tau_{kij} = \tau_{kj0} + \sum_{p=1}^{P} \tau_{kjp} x_{ip}. \tag{17}$$

Just as in any regression, there is an intercept to each of these equations.
These parameters, denoted v_{j0}, λ_{jm0}, and τ_{jk0} represent the predicted values of
intercepts, loadings, and thresholds, respectively, when all covariates are equal
to 0. The parameters v_{jp}, λ_{jmp}, and τ_{kjp} represent the predicted increment in the
intercept, loading, and threshold parameters associated with a one-unit increase
in covariate x_{ip}.

Just as between-person differences in the measurement parameters can be
modeled, so too can between-person differences in the latent variable's parameters itself – that is, latent variable mean and impact. Specifically, we can think
of the mean as a function of covariates as follows:

$$\alpha_{im} = \alpha_{0m} + \sum_{p=1}^{P} \alpha_{pm} x_{ip}. \tag{18}$$

Although it may be counterintuitive to think of each individual being characterized by their own mean (which is suggested by the presence of a subscript i for each value of α_{im}), we can instead think of α_{im} as the predicted value for individual i on latent variable m, given all their values of the covariates x_{ip}. We typically set α_{0m} to 0 for identification. If x_{ip} were a single grouping variable and there were no additional covariates, α_{pm} would be equivalent to the difference between groups in means. The difference here is that grouping variables represent just one of the types of covariates we can have. We refer to effects like this one as mean impact, as discussed above ("Differences that do not represent measurement bias").

Finally, we can also allow the variance of the latent variable to differ over levels of x_{ip} – that is, variance impact. This relation is parameterized in the same way as the other parameters, with one exception: because the variance must always be positive, we apply an exponential function as follows:

$$\psi_{im}^2 = \left(\psi_{0m} + \sum_{p=1}^{P} \psi_{pm} x_{ip} \right). \tag{19}$$

Because the exponential function yields a positive number in all cases, this alteration allows us to consistently model permissible values of ψ_{im}^2. As with α_{0m}, we typically set ψ_{0m} to zero for identification.

Note that regression-based models offer a major advantage over the multiple-groups formulation: they explicitly allow the incorporation of multiple covariates. Moreover, these covariates may be of any scale; they need not be grouping variables. Thus, in addition to the likelihood ratio test strategy outlined above, we can also simply test the significance of a given parameter. For instance, if there is a significant DIF effect of gender (which, for illustrative purposes, we will say is our first covariate; i.e., $p = 1$) on the intercept of Item 5, then the parameter ν_{51} will be significant.

A version of this model, the multiple indicator multiple cause (MIMIC; Finch, 2005; Muthén, 1989) model, introduced as the first major alternative to the multiple-groups formulation. In the MIMIC model, loading DIF (i.e., the equation for λ_{ijm}) is not allowed; nor is impact on the latent variable's variance (i.e., Equation 19). Thus, the MIMIC model generally models only uniform DIF and mean impact, and the model is best applied to cases where only differences in the overall levels of individual items are hypothesized. The full model, with all of the above equations, is typically referred to as moderated nonlinear factor analysis (MNLFA; Bauer, 2017; Bauer & Hussong, 2009). Because this is the most general instance of the model, we will move forward with this parameterization.

We fit a series of moderated nonlinear factor analyses to our example data using a specification search approach which is similar to the automated moderated nonlinear factor analysis (aMNLFA) algorithm described in greater detail later on ("Model-based approaches: specification searches"; Gottfredson et al., 2019). In our specification search, we fit one model for each item. In each of these models, all of the other items' measurement parameters (i.e., λ_{ijm}, ν_{ij}, and τ_{ijk} if estimated) are assumed noninvariant – that is, no between-participant differences are modeled for these items. For the focal item, the effects of all three covariates (parent gender, child sex, and child age) were modeled simultaneously. Note that, to offset the complexity of adding in multiple variables at once, we did not test between-person differences in thresholds τ_{ijk} here, only differences between intercepts ν_{ij}. As discussed below ("Model identification and anchor items"), a few additional constraints needed to be imposed to ensure model identification. In these models, we estimated each item's DIF model constraining the mean and variance of the latent variable to 0 and 1, respectively. This approach is not, however, the only identification strategy, as discussed below.

After fitting a series of item-wise models using the approach described above, we tallied all the DIF effects which were significant. We then combined these into a combined model, which contained (1) all of the DIF effects that were significant in the itemwise models, and (2) between-person differences in latent variable means and variances. In this penultimate model, the baseline value of the latent variable mean (α_0) and variance (ψ_0) were set to zero for identification purposes; the effects of all the covariates (i.e., α_g and ψ_g for all $g > 0$) were estimated. Note that we do retain some nonsignificant intercept effects in this model – for each loading we retain the corresponding intercept effect, as is standard to do whenever a loading effect is included. Further note that failing to include an intercept DIF effect in the presence of loading DIF would be much like including an interaction term without the corresponding main effect.

Finally, because the above model combines all the significant effects across items, a number of effects were rendered nonsignificant. Our final model removes any of the effects which were rendered nonsignificant in this penultimate model. Figure 10 shows this final model. When interpreting this figure, note that age was divided by 100 to facilitate model convergence. Because the model contains an exponential parameter (for the variance term), values of age in their original scale (weeks) caused estimation problems. In particular, because the number of weeks could often take the form of a relatively

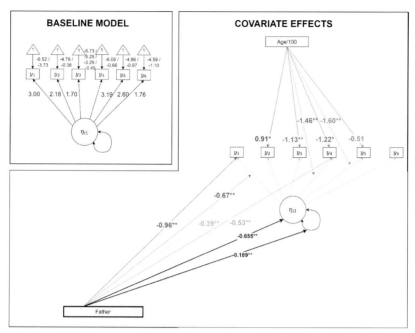

Figure 10 Final moderated nonlinear factor analysis model in our data example from the Longitudinal Study of Australian Children (LSAC; $N = 4,359$)

Note. To simplify presentation, the model is split into two diagrams: the baseline values of parameters, and the covariate effects. In the model for baseline measurement parameters, values of measurement parameters are shown for the case in which all covariates are equal to zero. Item thresholds are given next to the triangle for each item; for instance, the baseline threshold for endorsing the second and third response options for Item 1 is -8.52 and -3.73, respectively, in both groups. In the model for covariate effects, all effects for a given covariate-item pair are the same color; for instance, both the intercept and the loading effect for age on item y_4 are orange. Loading DIF is shown as a dotted line; intercept DIF is shown as a solid line. Finally, mean and variance impact are shown as bold black arrows. For all parameters, $**p < 0.01$, $*p < 0.05$, and $\dagger p < 0.10$.

large number (e.g., 60), the parameters associated with this form of age were often small enough (e.g., a 0.0001-unit shift in the variance of parental responsiveness, per week of age) that the covariance matrix of the parameters was difficult for the model to estimate. Dividing age by 100 put it on a similar scale to the other predictors, allowing us to circumvent issues with the parameter covariance matrix.

As shown in Figure 10, there were a number of DIF effects on intercepts v_{ij}. These are represented by arrows pointing from a covariate directly to an item. These effects represent the increment in log-odds in the probability of endorsing one category (i.e., category k) over the next category down (i.e., category $k-1$). For instance, the log-odds of endorsing a higher category (category 3 over category 2; category 2 over category 1) on Item 1 are 0.96 units lower among fathers than mothers. Parent gender shows a similar pattern of negative intercept effects on Items 3 and 4, indicating that fathers are less likely to endorse these items than mothers, even at the same level of responsiveness. Child age showed a less interpretable pattern of intercept effects, with a positive effect on the intercept of Item 2 but negative effects on Item 3; note that some nonsignificant effects of age are included, corresponding to loading effects on the same items.

Figure 10 also shows a number of DIF effects on loadings λ_{ij}, depicted as arrows pointing to other arrows. They represent the increment in log-odds in the value of λ_{ij} associated with a one-unit shift in the variable. For instance, the loading for Item 4 decreases by 1.46 units for every 100-week increase in child age (or 0.0146 units for every week increase), indicating a weaker relation between this item and responsive parenting among parents of older children. A similar effect was seen for Item 5, which was also more weakly related to the latent variable among parents of older children. A negative loading effect was seen for parent gender on Item 2, which showed a weaker relation to responsive parenting among fathers than mothers.

Finally, with respect to the latent variable, Figure 10 shows that fathers were both less responsive overall and more variable in their responsiveness than mothers. The lower overall level of responsive parenting among fathers is indicated by the negative mean impact effect. Note that it is challenging to interpret the magnitude of this effect given that the variance impact parameter is also significant; there is no unit in which the coefficient of -0.655 can be placed. Thus, we cannot say that fathers are, for instance, -0.655 standard deviations lower in responsiveness than mothers – we simply know that they are significantly lower. The positive variance effect indicates that fathers showed higher levels of variability in their responsiveness. It represents the increment in log-odds of the variance associated with being a father, relative to being a mother. Following Equation 19, we say that the variance of responsive parenting was 1 in mothers and $e^{0.189} = 1.21$ in fathers.

5.5 Model Identification and Anchor Items

As noted when we first introduced the common factor model in Equation 1, a number of constraints typically need to be imposed on parameters for a latent variable model to be identified. Ensuring model identification becomes even more complicated when we allow for between-person differences in measurement parameters (i.e., DIF) and latent variable means and variances (i.e., impact).

One possibility is to constrain the latent variable's mean and variance to 0 and 1 respectively, across all participants. In the multiple-groups formulation, this would be equivalent to setting α_{mg} to zero and ψ^2_{mg} to 1 for all values of g and m. In a regression-based formulation, it would be equivalent to simply setting α_{im} to 0 and ψ^2_{im} to 1 for all participants –that is, not estimating any regression effects (i.e., α_{pm} or ψ_{pm}) and simply constraining α_{0m} and ψ^2_{0m} to 0 and 1. The disadvantages of this approach are clear: if there are in fact differences between participants in the means and variances (which, in practice, is often both true and of primary interest), this model will not capture them.

Another possibility is to constrain one item's loading λ_{jm} and intercept v_j to 1 and 0 across all individuals. As with the case of latent variable means and variances discussed above, the parameters associated with this strategy differ between multiple-groups and regression-based approaches. However, in both cases, this is essentially the same as the "reference item" approach in factor analysis more generally, but now it carries an additional implication: this item's measurement parameters are also assumed to be equal across groups.

Alternatively, there are a number of options which combine the features of these two strategies. One possible approach combines the following two constraints.

1. First, the value of the latent variable's mean and variance are set to 0 and 1 for some baseline value of a DIF-generating covariate. In the multiple-groups case, the factor means and variances for the reference group, α_{m0} and ψ^2_{m0}, are set to 0 and 1, and the corresponding values in the other groups are estimated freely. In regression-based approaches, baseline values α_{0m} and ψ^2_{0m} are set to 0 (with a value of 0 for ψ^2_{0m} corresponding to a variance of 1, given the exponential term in Equation 19), while all regression coefficients α_{pm} and $\psi^2_{pm}, p \neq 0$ are estimated freely. This strategy allows the researcher to estimate impact, while setting a common scale for the latent variable.

2. Second, set one item on which is invariant across levels of each DIF-generating covariate. In multiple-groups models this means that there must be an item whose measurement parameters (including loadings, intercepts, and thresholds, if included) do not vary across groups. In regression-based formulations, this means that, for each covariate x_{ip}, there must be at least one item on which x_{ip} has no DIF effect (loading, intercept, or threshold).

When the above two conditions are met, the multiple-groups and regression-based models are generally identified. This approach is the model identification strategy we have used with the example data in multiple-group formulation discussed earlier in the Element.

Note that, like the reference item strategy mentioned above, this set of constraints does require at least one item to be invariant across all participants. This item is called the *anchor item*. Though the terms "reference item" and "anchor item" are sometimes used interchangeably, here we will use the former term to refer to any item whose loading and intercept are set to 0 and 1 respectively, and the latter term to refer to any item whose parameters are constrained to equality across participants. In other words, an anchor item's measurement parameters are estimated freely, with the only requirement being that they do not vary across participants.

A few considerations are important to note. First, recall that all of these different identification strategies result in the same model fit. Neither is "better" than the other; any one of these may be preferable depending on the researcher's goals and interests. Second, note that a few different constraints must be applied in the case of nonlinear models (see Millsap & Yun-Tein, 2004 for details). For example, if thresholds τ_{jk} are being estimated, all of the thresholds τ_{jk} and intercepts v_j are not jointly identified, as noted above; at least one threshold, or v_j, must be set to zero.

Finally, note that in general, unless we set all latent variable parameters to be equal across participants (which, again, is generally an untenable assumption), there must always be at least one anchor item. However, this raises an obvious issue: what happens if the researcher chooses an anchor item (or, if the loading and intercept are set to 0 and 1, reference item) which is actually noninvariant? In the context of specification searches (discussed below: "Model-based methods: specification searches"), there is substantial evidence that choosing an anchor item which is actually noninvariant may cause both type I and type II errors, leading the researcher to erroneously find DIF and miss DIF which is actually present (Cheung & Rensvold, 1999; Meade & Wright, 2012; Raykov et al., 2020).

Researchers have proposed a number of ways to get around this issue. First, before testing alternate models (as was done in both the data examples above), we could perform a preliminary specification search to find an appropriate anchor item before proceeding to further tests. One proposed solution is an iterative factor ratio testing procedure, which essentially tests every possible combination of anchor and DIF-generating items (Cheung & Rensvold, 1999). Although this strategy is comprehensive, it does become more challenging to find DIF as the number of noninvariant items increases; this is particularly the case if all of the DIF effects are in the same direction (Meade & Lautenschlager, 2004; Yoon & Millsap, 2007). A less time-consuming and computationally intensive approach is to test itemwise models, as was done in the regression-based modeling example above, and rank items in order of their likelihood ratio test statistic, choosing the one with the smallest value as the anchor item (Woods, 2009a). These are only a few of the strategies we could use to identify anchor items, and readers are referred to two comprehensive reviews (Kopf et al., 2015a, 2015b) for greater detail. We also discuss a new class of modeling approaches which do not require anchor items below ("Approximate approaches").

6 Consequences of Measurement Noninvariance and Differential Item Functioning

Having established all of the ways we can model noninvariance or DIF, it makes sense to revisit the question of why we would want to do so in the first place. Although we of course understand that bias from person-level background covariates is undesirable, we can understand at a more granular level what the specific consequences of each type of measurement noninvariance will be in terms of the inferences that can be drawn. As it turns out, different fields also have different ideas about the consequences of DIF, and the recourse we have if DIF is found. Moreover, there are a few issues which may have somewhat different ramifications in theory than in practice.

6.1 Ramifications for the Interpretations of Between-Groups Comparisons

Within the SEM framework, the question of measurement invariance has historically been framed in terms of the validity of between-group comparisons: at a given level of invariance, what between-group comparisons can be made? Absent configural invariance, no comparisons can be made at all; a lack of configural invariance implies that entirely different constructs are being measured in the two groups. Thus, to attempt to compare the groups in terms of any of the latent variables would be incoherent.

If metric invariance – equivalence across all items in λ_{jm} – is not satisfied, between-group comparisons in the covariance structure of the latent variable cannot be made. The inability to compare covariance structures between groups means that any inferences about relations among variables – including structural equation model results but also regression coefficients – cannot be compared across groups. Of course, the issue of partial invariance – the idea that some, but not all, measurement parameters may be invariant – complicates this rule.

One argument (Byrne et al., 1989) holds that even in the case of some factor loadings being noninvariant, thus causing the researcher to reject the hypothesis of complete metric invariance across all items in Y, some cross-group comparisons may be made as long as noninvariant items are in the minority. The authors, as well as others in later work (Steenkamp and Baumgartner, 1998), further argue that if cross-validation work supports the tests' validity, a lack of metric invariance can often be considered an artifact of the sample.

If scalar invariance – equivalence across groups in v_j – is not satisfied, between-group comparisons in latent variable means cannot be made (Bollen, 1989). This finding was particularly important one in the original context in which measurement invariance analyses were first conducted, because erroneous conclusions of differences between group means (e.g., differences in mean intelligence among members of different races) were often based on findings of differences between groups in mean scores (Millsap, 1998). In many ways, such conclusions were the *raison d'etre* of measurement invariance analysis – by showing that a scale lacked scalar invariance, researchers could show that between group means in this scale were a function of differences in item intercepts (i.e., v_j) as opposed to differences in the latent variable.

Implicit in these prohibitions on cross-group comparisons are equally stringent prohibitions on cross-group generalization: findings cannot be generalized from one group to another in the absence of measurement invariance. For instance, suppose that a regression links one variable to another in a given group, but the metric invariance assumption is not satisfied for at least one of the variables. Then these regression findings cannot be generalized to the other group.

6.2 Ramifications for the Accuracy of Factor Scores

In many applications, the principal goal of applying IRT or factor analysis is to obtain some estimate of a subject's overall level of the latent variable. Perhaps the most common method is obtaining a sum score for each individual by summing their responses to each item. There are a number of issues associated with sum scores, including their failure to take into account measurement error and implicit assumption that all items load equally onto the factor (McNeish & Wolf, 2020). However, with respect to the question of measurement invariance specifically, one issue becomes obvious: if there is DIF in any item, this DIF will be directly incorporated into the sum score. For instance, suppose that we are working with continuous items, and all but one item, item j, are invariant across groups. For this item the value of v_j is 1.5 units higher in group 1, relative to group 2. If we create sum scores, these sum scores will be on average 1.5 units higher in group 1 than group 2.

For this and many other reasons, it is preferable to obtain estimates of the latent variable for each participant that incorporate information from the model. These estimates, which we can denote $\hat{\eta}_{im}$, are referred to as *factor scores* (Grice, 2001). After the latent variable model is estimated, the parameters are then used to generate estimates of $\hat{\eta}_{im}$, which can then be used in subsequent analyses. Importantly, while it may intuitively seem as though there is only one possible value for each person which fits in the model laid out above, in actuality there are an infinite number of sets of η_{im} values for all N participants which work in a given model. Accordingly, there are many ways in which to calculate factor scores $\hat{\eta}_{im}$. While a full review of factor score calculation methods is beyond the scope of this Element, we note that modal a posteriori (MAP), expected a posteriori (EAP), and plausible value-based scores are three common types of scores arising from the IRT literature (Fischer & Rose, 2019; Muraki & Engelhard Jr, 1985). There are a number of equivalencies between these methods of calculating factor scores and methods arising from the factor analysis literature which work with continuous indicators, such as Bartlett scores and regression factor scores (DiStefano et al., 2009; Skrondal & Laake, 2001), but we do not review them here.

Because estimates of $\hat{\eta}_{im}$ are obtained from estimates of the parameters, it stands to reason that bias in the parameters will lead to biases in factor scores. As discussed earlier, strict invariance is often untenable in practice – but in the case of continuous items, it is theoretically necessary if we want to obtain completely unbiased estimates of $\hat{\eta}_{im}$ (Millsap, 1997, 1998). In practice, however, the effects of measurement noninvariance/DIF on factor scores are much less certain than this.

6.3 Empirical Findings: Does DIF Actually Matter?

We can make a variety of predictions about the consequences of DIF, based on the known mathematical relations among different model parameters as discussed above. However, even though it is in theory a mathematically demonstrable fact that, for instance, higher values of v_j in one group will lead to overestimated values of the latent variable means in that group, the actual consequences in real data are unknown. Thus, a large and growing body of research focuses on establishing whether and to what extent DIF biases estimates of between-group differences, as well as scores on the latent variable itself.

With respect to differences between groups, it has been demonstrated that differences across groups in factor loadings and intercepts may indeed lead to erroneous findings of between-group differences in means and covariance structures (Chen, 2007; French & Finch, 2006; Millsap, 1997). As we might expect, such differences are generally in proportion to the magnitude of the DIF observed, in terms of both the proportion of items with DIF and the size of the DIF effects themselves. Additionally, in the case of multiple groups, sample size differences can lead to less severe bias in the larger group and more severe bias in the smaller group (Chen, 2008; Millsap & Kwok, 2004). However, it is critical to note that such biases are generally observed only in cases in which the estimated model does not account for DIF. That is to say, when models which model partial noninvariance such as the multiple groups and regression-based models shown above are fit, and the DIF effects which are truly present are accounted for by the model, estimates of differences between groups in latent variable means, variances, and covariances are generally unbiased (French & Finch, 2006; Millsap & Kwok, 2004).

Although it is clear that sum scores for each individual will not be correct in the presence of measurement noninvariance, the magnitude of the issues caused by sum scores in subsequent analyses is more difficult to quantify, as the accuracy of any score must be considered relative to the context in which it is being used (Millsap & Kwok, 2004). Selection represents one context in which sum scores arising from noninvariant items can cause a substantial problem. That is, when researchers create sum scores and use some cut point as a selection criterion, the sensitivity and specificity of such criteria may be reduced substantially by measurement noninvariance (Lai et al., 2021; Lai et al., 2022; Millsap & Kwok, 2004). Additionally, when sum scores are used in mean comparisons, Type I error rates (e.g., of t-tests) are inflated in the presence of noninvariance (Li & Zumbo, 2009). This bias has been shown to be more pronounced if intercepts are noninvariant, relative to loadings (Steinmetz, 2013).

Findings are considerably more complicated when it comes to the accuracy of individual factor scores, $\hat{\eta}_{im}$. A growing body of research investigates this question by simulating data with DIF, fitting a model which fails to account for DIF or accounts for it incompletely, and examining the relation between the true and estimated values of the latent variable for each participant. Under some circumstances, failing to model DIF may be problematic. With binary items, simulation work has shown that failing to account for DIF in estimating factor scores could yield biased estimates of the relations between these factor scores and covariates in subsequent analyses (Curran et al., 2018). However, misspecifying the nature of DIF in the model which is used to estimate factor scores may be less of a problem – in other words, as long as some covariate effects on items are estimated, it is not always critical to get the location of these effects correct. Evidence for this is provided by simulation studies which find correlations in excess of $r = 0.9$ between factor scores from misspecified models and their true values (Chalmers et al., 2016; Curran et al., 2016). Additionally, some work using empirical data has shown that models which specify different DIF effects often yield factor scores which are very similar (Cole et al., 2022). However, as noted above, the context in which factor scores are to be used is critical. In some high-stakes settings such as state and federal educational testing, two sets of factor scores which are correlated at $r = 0.95$ are not sufficiently similar to be interchangeable.

7 Detecting Measurement Noninvariance and Differential Item Functioning

The entirety of our discussion thus far has sidestepped one major issue: the pattern of DIF effects is rarely known in advance. We often have many items, many covariates, and few substantive hypotheses about where and even whether DIF exists in our dataset. Even with a standard number of items and covariates, the number of possible covariate-item pairs that need to be investigated for DIF may become unmanageable. For example, with four covariates and ten items, there are 40 possible covariate-item DIF pairs. Add to this the fact that DIF must be estimated on a specific parameter (e.g., loadings, thresholds, intercepts) and that all possible DIF effects may be combined into any number of models, and the number of choices becomes orders of magnitude larger. The rest of this Element focuses on different ways for determining the location and magnitude of DIF effects in our sample.

As we will see shortly, there are many such methods. Recent work (Lai et al., 2021) distinguishes between two different types of methods for locating DIF: *specification search* approaches and *approximate invariance* approaches. The former approach involves testing a set of models with different DIF effects in a prespecified order, conducting repeated model comparisons with the goal of finding the model with the best fit. These models are akin to stepwise regression algorithms, in that they entail repeated applications of models which themselves are estimated in the "typical" way, typically full information maximum likelihood. That is, there is nothing in the estimation algorithm which maximizes simplicity; the standard algorithm is simply applied repeatedly with different constraints. By contrast, approximate invariance methods seek to minimize the overall number of meaningfully large DIF effects in the model. They constrain the complexity using a penalty parameter, which may be incorporated in a variety of different ways. We review specific subtypes of these methods, drawing comparisons and contrasts both within and between these broad classifications.

Table 5 Decision-making guide for all of the DIF detection methods in the Element

Method	Indicator type			Unit of analysis	Type of model		Software availability			Other considerations
	Binary	Ordinal	Continuous		Multiple groups	Regression-based	Mplus	R	Amos	
Pre-estimation										
Mantel-Haenszel	Yes	Yes	No – have to bin	Item	Yes	No	No	Yes	No	Higher Type I error rate than SIBTEST.
Logistic regression	Yes	Yes	No	Item	No	Yes	No	Yes	No	Higher Type I error rate than SIBTEST.
SIBTEST	Yes	Yes	No – have to bin	Item	Yes	No	No	Yes	No	Multiple different adaptations of SIBTEST, including crossing and non-crossing (see, e.g., Chalmers, 2018).
Specification searches										
CFA-based methods	Possible	Possible	Typical	Test	Yes	No	Yes	Yes	Yes	Note that to consider configural invariance, multiple groups are required.
IRT-LR-DIF	Typical	Typical	Possible	Item	Yes	Yes	Yes	Yes	No	Parameterized in Mplus through MODEL CONSTRAINT.
aMNLFA	Typical	Typical	Possible	Item	Possible	Yes	Yes	Yes	No	Parameterized in Mplus through MODEL CONSTRAINT.
Wald-adjusted method of Woods et al. (2013)	Typical	Typical	Possible	Item	Yes	No	Yes	Yes	No	Parameterized in Mplus through MODEL CONSTRAINT.

Approximate approaches										
Regularization	Typical	Typical	Typical	Item	Yes	No	No	Yes	No	Currently only able to accommodate listwise deletion of missing data.
Alignment	Typical	Typical	Typical	Item	No	Yes	Yes	No	No	Multiple different loss functions to choose from, as well as Bayesian and frequentist versions; decisions not reviewed here.
Effect sizes										
DTFR	Yes	Yes	Yes	Test	Yes	No	No	Yes	No	
dMACS	No	No	Yes	Item	Yes	No	No	Yes	No	
Signed	dMACS	No	No	Yes	Item	Yes	Yes	No	Yes	No
Indices summarized by Chalmers (2023)	Yes	Yes	No	Item	Yes	No	No	Yes	No	
Adjusted indices in Gunn et al. (2020)	No	No	No	Item	Yes	No	No	Yes	No	These adjust for differences in latent variable distributions.
wABC	Yes	Yes	No	Item	Yes	No	No	Yes	No	

We also include a set of measures which seek to detect DIF outside the estimation of the DIF model itself. In particular, these testing procedures obtain approximate indicators of the location of DIF effects without actually estimating a latent variable model; these are typically employed for the purpose of finding unsuitable items before fitting a model in the first place. We denote these methods *pre-estimation* approaches to finding DIF.

7.1 Organization of This Section

As noted above, the majority of this section will focus on three broad groupings of DIF detection strategies: premodel approaches, specification searches, and approximate invariance methods. We will also briefly discuss *effect size* measures as a supplement to DIF detection procedures. At the end of each section we will review the evidence for all the different subtypes of each method and provide recommendations. All methods are summarized in Table 5, to which we will refer throughout each section. Finally, many of these methods were developed for cases in which there is only one latent variable, and are sufficiently computationally intensive that they are often not run on multiple latent variables at once. Thus, we will consider only the univariate case throughout the section, revisiting the case of multiple latent variables at the end of the section. Thus, the subscript m, which had previously been used to index latent variables, will be dropped.

7.2 Pre-estimation Approaches

There are a number of testing procedures for finding DIF which do not depend on the estimation of a model itself. That is, given only participants' observed responses, we can calculate a number of effect size indices, and in some cases conduct inferential tests, which give insight into whether and where DIF may be present. We refer to these as *pre-estimation* approaches. In general, they use a proxy for the latent variable η_i to assess each item for DIF in advance of running the model. The methods we will review are summarized in the top few rows of Table 5.

If pre-estimation approaches have not yet estimated a model for η_i, how are they able to detect DIF or determine whether the scale measuring η_i is invariant? Most of these tests instead work with a sum-score of items, S_i. The basic premise of a sum score test for DIF is that S_i may serve as a proxy for η_i and the relation between S_i and an item y_{ij} should be invariant across groups – i.e., $P(y_{ij}|S_i, g) = P(y_{ij}|S_i)$.

One of the first of these tests is the Mantel–Haenszel (Holland & Thayer, 1986; Zwick, 1990). The sum score variable S_i is stratified into Q levels, with each group being defined as s_q. Then the M–H tests the following null hypothesis:

$$H0 : \frac{P(y_{ij} = 1|S_i = s_q, G = 1)/P(y_{ij} = 0|S_i = s_q, G = 1)}{P(y_{ij} = 1|S_i = s_q, G = 0)/P(y_{ij} = 0|S_i = s_q, G = 0)} = \alpha = 1 \tag{20}$$

for all K groups. Here, α represents the ratio of the probability of a "correct" response (i.e., $y_{ij} = 1$) at a given level of the sum score in Group 1, to the same quantity in Group 0. The estimate of this quantity $\hat{\alpha}$ can be obtained by:

$$\hat{\alpha} = \frac{\sum_k (A_q D_q)/N_q}{\sum_k (B_q C_q)/N_q}, \tag{21}$$

where A_q and B_q are the number of subjects in group $g = 1$ who answer item y_{ij} correctly and incorrectly respectively, and C_q and D_q are the number of subjects in group $g = 0$ who answer item y_{ij} correctly and incorrectly respectively. In testing the null hypothesis that the odds of a correct response do not differ on the basis of group membership across all levels of S_q, the M–H test only considers uniform DIF. Additionally, by stratifying the sum score S_i into groups s_q, the M–H procedure obscures information about continuous variation in the data. A sum-score procedure which corrects these deficiencies is logistic regression procedure (Swaminathan & Rogers, 1990). Like the M–H procedure, the logistic regression procedure uses S_i as a stand-in for η_i, but it does so without grouping values of S_i, and treating values of S_i as a regressor in a logistic regression equation as follows:

$$logit(y_{ij}) = \tau_0 + \tau_1 S_i + \tau_2 g + \tau_3 S_i g. \tag{22}$$

The logic of this test is that, should there be no DIF between items based on groupings g, there should be no association between y_{ij} and g, or the interaction between S_i and g, after controlling for S_i. A significant main effect of g indicates uniform DIF, whereas a significant interaction effect indicates nonuniform DIF.

The simultaneous item bias test (SIBTEST) procedure is based on logic similar to the logistic regression and Mantel–Haenszel procedures, developing on these approaches in a number of ways (Shealy & Stout, 1993). As noted above, sum score methods such as M–H and logistic regression assume that sum scores are a suitable proxy for the latent variable. Using sum scores as a proxy for the latent variable makes sense by many reasonable arguments. In particular, because a sum score is simply an unweighted sum, a method which uses sum scores implicitly assumes that items all load equally onto the latent variable (i.e., $\lambda_j = \lambda_h$ for all j and h). In this way sum score methods map very well onto a type of model called a Rasch model (Bond et al., 2020). These models do actually hold all loadings constant, modeling all differences between items using a variety of other parameters (including, but not limited to, the intercept and threshold parameters we have discussed so far). Thus, in a setting in which a Rasch model is appropriate, we may find sum score methods totally adequate.

However, the use of sum scores entails many assumptions that may not be satisfied. First, in many cases the assumption of equal loadings just mentioned simply is not true (e.g., McNeish & Wolf, 2020). Although Rasch models may be totally appropriate for a number of cases, developmental scientists often find ourselves in research scenarios in which there is plenty of reason to assume loadings differ across items. Second, sum score methods also implicitly assume that the sum score itself contains no DIF, because the very items in which we are testing DIF are incorporated into the sum score – but of course, we would not be testing for DIF if we thought this assumption were satisfied.

Finally, though this is not an assumption of all sum score methods, the simultaneous item bias test (SIBTEST) improves on earlier "standardization"-based methods (Dorans & Kulick, 1986), which did not take into account the possibility that there were differences between groups in the distribution of the latent variables. SIBTEST estimates a measure of DIF across the entire distribution of the latent variable, $\hat{\beta}$, as follows:

$$\hat{\beta} = \sum_{j=1}^{J} p_j \left(\bar{Y}_{Fj}^* - \bar{Y}_{Rj}^* \right). \tag{23}$$

Here, p_j is the proportion of participants providing a given answer to item j – for example, the proportion of participants providing a response of 0 or 1 to a binary item. For the reference and focal groups, respectively, $\bar{Y}_{Rj}^*$ and $\bar{Y}_{Fj}^*$ are essentially an adjusted value of a participant's entire scale score given their value of j. We do not explain how this adjustment works here, directing readers to elsewhere for more detail (DeMars, 2009; Jiang & Stout, 1998), but this adjustment is sometimes referred to as a "regression adjustment" or "regression correction," which estimates the reliability of each item to obtain an estimate of the true score for a participant at that level of the item. This estimate of the true score is then used in a Taylor series approximation to obtain the predicted score on $\bar{Y}$ at that value of the true score (Jiang & Stout, 1998).

A full description of this computation will not be given here, but the reader is referred elsewhere for a comprehensive, accessible explanation of the equations (DeMars, 2009). For our purposes, the point is that the simultaneous item bias (SIBTEST) approach allows comparisons between the focal and reference group on each item, conditional on an estimate of participants' true scores. The adjustments made by the SIBTEST approach allow for greater precision, including decreased Type 1 error rates (Jodoin & Gierl, 2001; Roussos & Stout, 1996), relative to observed-score methods such as M–H and logistic regression.

Additionally, there are methods of calculating the standard error of $\hat{\beta}$, allowing researchers to test the null hypothesis that DIF is absent.

7.2.1 Findings and Recommendations

In general, with respect to pre-estimation approaches, findings from Monte Carlo simulations indicate that the "regression adjustment" employed by the simultaneous item bias (SIBTEST) strategy yields less inflated Type I error rates than the logistic regression and Mantel–Haenszel procedures (Jiang & Stout, 1998; Li & Stout, 1996; Roussos & Stout, 1996). However, even within SIBTEST there are multiple different methods of computing $\hat{\beta}$. Some, for instance, are better suited to "crossing" DIF, or nonuniform DIF as discussed earlier. Two of the most substantial determinants of SIBTEST's outperformance of logistic regression and Mantel–Haenszel are (1) the degree to which factor loadings differ across items, and (2) the extent of the differences between groups in their latent means (DeMars, 2009). This caveat is important to note because, for many research contexts, SIBTEST will not be possible: because it can only be applied to multiple-groups formulations and not continuous covariates, there will be cases in which SIBTEST cannot be used. When multiple covariates, or a continuous covariate, are under consideration, we must use the logistic regression formulation; this is the only one of the pretest methods which can accommodate regression-based models.

7.3 Model-Based Methods: Specification Searches

In the multiple-groups and regression-based approaches discussed above ("Models for measurement invariance and DIF"), DIF is incorporated directly into the model. For both multiple groups and regression-based approaches, specification search methods test a series of models against one another in order to determine the pattern of DIF effects. In multiple-groups methods, models which include DIF on some items on the basis of a given grouping variable are tested against some baseline model. This general strategy raises two main issues. First, there is the question of what constitutes an appropriate baseline model to which to compare a model which includes DIF. Second, as discussed above ("Model identification and anchor items"), there is a need to hold some items invariant across groups, in order to connect the metric of η_i across groups. Differences both within and between IRT and SEM in conventions around choosing anchor items have been well-established (e.g., Stark et al., 2006).

Most regression-based formulations follow a similar logic to this multiple-groups approach. Instead of testing differences in model fit, regression-based specification searches generally involve testing the significance of parameter estimates. Thus, because there is no baseline model per se, the two issues raised in the previous paragraph are one and the same in a regression-based approach: we must simply decide which DIF effects to estimate and which to constrain.

The methods outlined below, thus, can involve either a multiple-groups or a regression-based parameterization. For brevity and ease of presentation, we present them according to a multiple-groups parameterization, without loss of generality. The methods we will review are summarized in the middle section of Table 5.

7.3.1 Starting from a Maximally Constrained Model: IRT-LR-DIF

The most prominent specification search procedure arising from IRT is the likelihood ratio test (IRT-LR-DIF; Thissen, 2001), which is formulated as follows Although the LR in IRT-LR-DIF stands for "logistic regression," the entire acronym itself does not have a name. As such, we will continue to refer to it as the "likelihood ratio test" throughout this Element, always putting IRT-LR-DIF in parentheses afterward to avoid confusion with the general likelihood ratio testing approach mentioned earlier. The steps are as follows:

1. Set the mean and variance of η_{ij} in the one group to 0 and 1 respectively; allow the corresponding mean and variance in all other groups.
2. Allow the loading and intercept for item j to differ between groups – that is, set $\lambda_{j0} \neq \lambda_{j1} \neq \ldots \neq \lambda_{jG}$ and $v_{j0} \neq v_{j1} \neq \ldots \neq v_{jG}$.
3. Set item parameters equal between groups for all other items – that is, set $\lambda_{h0} = \lambda_{h1} = \ldots = \lambda_{hG}$ and $v_{h0} = v_{h1} = v_{hG}, h \neq j$.

In other words, this model has DIF on only one item, on the basis of all groups; the parameters λ_j and v_j (and, if present, τ_{kj}) are constrained across groups. This model is then compared to a model with no DIF on any of the items, using the likelihood ratio test strategy described above. A significant test statistic indicates that a model with item j's item parameters allowed to freely vary across groups is a better fit to the data than a model in which item j's parameters are invariant – that is, a significant result indicates that item j shows DIF. This test is repeated for all items, which necessitates controlling for multiple comparisons; this may be done using the Benjamini-Hochberg procedure (Thissen et al., 2002). Additionally, if DIF is found for a given item at the omnibus level (i.e., either λ_j or v_j differs across groups) post-hoc comparisons may be conducted to determine which parameter shows DIF. A number of extensions of this procedure exist, including modifications which allow η_i to be non-normal in one or both groups (Woods, 2008).

Within the SEM framework, multiple groups testing for MI, as expressed through invariance across groups of elements of Λ, τ, and Σ, follows a very different order, both starting from a different baseline model and proceeding through the testing of parameters differently. Whereas DIF testing procedures tend to start from the most restrictive model, MI testing procedures more often start from the least restrictive model, allowing a maximum of items to vary across levels of G. The baseline model may be constrained so that all elements of $\Lambda_1 \neq \Lambda_2 \neq \ldots \neq \Lambda_{NG}$ and $\tau_1 \neq \tau_2 \neq \ldots \neq \tau_{NG}$, with the only exception of a constraint to guarantee model identification. As in a single-group factor analysis, perhaps most common is the solution referent item having its value of λ_j or τ_j set to 1 in both groups for identification of the metric (i.e., the "reference item" strategy noted above; Reise et al., 1993).

With respect to parameter types, many (e.g., Steenkamp & Baumgartner, 1998; Vandenberg & Lance, 2000) propose testing the invariance of factor loadings before intercepts, and only testing the invariance of intercepts for which factor loadings are equivalent. In fact, the canonical way to apply this procedure tests the models in the order in which they are shown in Figure 3: configural invariance, then metric invariance, then scalar invariance, and then (if possible) strict invariance (not shown in Figure 3). The logic here is that, because metric invariance is a precursor to scalar invariance, an item with noninvariant factor loadings is problematic regardless of whether its intercept parameter is invariant. Note the stark contrast between this method and the likelihood ratio test (IRT-LR-DIF) procedure reviewed in the previous section, in which invariance of λ_j and ν_j are tested simultaneously.

In general, we would typically test these models against one another using the likelihood ratio tests described above. However, given that these models are generally fit with standard SEM software, a plethora of fit indices may be consulted, with the CFI, RMSEA, and SRMR suggested as highly sensitive fit indices (Cheung & Rensvold, 2002b); however, the SRMR might be more sensitive to differences in factor loadings than intercepts or residual covariance matrices (Chen, 2007). We may also theoretically consult modification indices to determine which items are noninvariant (Reise et al., 1993; Yoon & Kim, 2014). However, problems with modification indices are well-documented, including potential capitalization on chance, as well as the subjectivity of whether a given modification index qualifies as sufficiently large to be problematic.

A number of specification search approaches seek to find a middle ground between these approaches, typically by imposing slightly different combinations of parameter constraints to ensure that no DIF is erroneously found or missed due to model misspecification. For instance, in the two-group case, one adjusted model implements a Wald test, which estimates first (1) a constrained model with no DIF, with group 1's mean and variance constrained to 0 and 1 respectively, and group 2's mean and variance are freely estimated; and then (2) a model with group 2's mean and variance constrained to their estimated value from step (1) and all item parameters allowed to vary freely (Woods et al., 2013). This sequence of steps helps to ensure that the results are robust to potential misspecification of between-group differences in the latent variable distribution.

Another method arises from regression-based approaches to nonlinear factor analyses, particularly moderated nonlinear factor analysis (MNLFA). As MNLFA has become more widely used, algorithms for determining the location of impact and DIF have evolved to match the complexity of MNLFA models and the questions they aim to answer. Perhaps the best-known is the set of steps instantiated in the automated MNLFA (aMNLFA) procedure and accompanying R package aMNLFA (Curran et al., 2014; Gottfredson et al., 2019). Given P covariates and J items measuring a single latent variable (assuming the same covariates are used for DIF and impact for simplicity), the procedure is summarized as follows.

1. The likelihood ratio test (IRT-LR-DIF) procedure is followed, with all covariates being added to the model at once using a regression formulation (i.e., each item is regressed on multiple covariates). Mean and variance impact on covariates are also included at this stage.
2. All significant ($p < 0.05$) DIF and impact effects are then collected into a single model to estimate simultaneously.
3. A Benjamini-Hochberg correction for multiple comparisons is then performed, and any DIF and impact effects which remain are retained (Thissen et al., 2002).

Note that this procedure is explicitly designed to incorporate multiple covariates, unlike most of the procedures we have discussed thus far. The potential benefits and challenges of this approach are discussed in the next section. We used a procedure very similar to this one in the preceding example, resulting in the model shown in Figure 10.

7.3.4 Findings and Recommendations

There are a number of considerations which inform a researcher's choice when conducting specification searches. First, the probability of both type I and type II errors must be considered. One might expect significant effects to be found by the likelihood ratio test (IRT-LR-DIF) at much smaller sample sizes than the minimally constrained configural invariance model, as the large number of parameters in the latter approach can reduce one's power to find DIF effects (Xu & Green, 2016). Indeed, the IRT-LR-DIF procedure has shown adequate power and adequate control of type I error rates even under small sample sizes. In the two-group setting, performance has been relatively strong with group sizes of roughly $N = 300$ in the case of equally sized groups (Woods, 2009b). There is some evidence from simulation studies that when using the minimally constrained approach sample sizes of $N = 200$ or $N = 300$ in each group can yield acceptable power, but only under certain conditions such as when outcomes are normally distributed, there are many response variables, or the overall level of DIF is high. The wide-ranging nature of these conditions underscores an important point when comparing specification search approaches, which is that the statistical power of DIF tests depends on many factors aside from sample size, often in combination with one another. In particular, DIF effects will generally be easier to find when there are more items and DIF effects are large (e.g., French & Finch, 2006; Meade et al., 2008; Woods, 2009b). Additionally, power to detect DIF with normally distributed items is often greater than that to detect DIF with binary or ordinal items (French & Finch, 2006).

One issue a researcher will almost definitely confront when choosing a specification search approach is model misspecification. Given that each of these specification searches involves fitting multiple models, at least one of the models fit under these procedures is likely to be misspecified. The maximally constrained model, which is the starting point for the likelihood ratio test (IRT-LR-DIF), is misspecified if even one item aside from the focal item is noninvariant. There is substantial evidence that this can be problematic, particularly given that the χ^2 test will yield biased results if the baseline model is not correct (Maydeu-Olivares & Cai, 2006) – which, of course, it likely will be given how stringent its constraints are. However, although the minimally constrained configural model with which SEM-based approaches typically start will almost by definition provide a closer fit to the data than the maximally constrained model used in IRT-LR-DIF, even in the maximally constrained model, model misspecification is still a major concern.

In this spirit, based on the sensitivity and specificity of each of these specification searches, as well as the possibility that they may disagree, it is recommended that researchers try at least two different types of specification search methods and assess the agreement between them before proceeding. There is no one procedure which is definitively superior to the others based on prior evidence. It is well-known that, when they are applied carelessly, purely data-driven searches can lead to nonsensical results in SEM; thus, researchers must be thoughtful and retain only effects which are consistent with theory and hold up across multiple different testing methods (MacCallum et al., 1992). Moreover, specification searches arguably incur more researcher degrees of freedom than any other method, given the number of choices each specific procedure entails. Results from multiverse analyses (Cole et al., 2022) indicate that even small data-management decisions can substantially impact the results of these searches, further underscoring the importance of taking care when applying these methods.

7.4 Approximate Approaches

Finally, approximate approaches attempt to arrive at a solution which balances fit and parsimony by altering standard estimation algorithms to penalize an excess of DIF parameters. These are in general the newest and most computationally intensive approaches, but they show great promise in helping researchers to find DIF effects in a maximally data-driven way without incurring many of the problems of specification searches. The methods we will review are summarized in Table 5.

7.4.1 Regularization

When fitting regression models, it is frequently the case that there are many possible covariates and the researcher has no a priori hypotheses about which effects are truly meaningful. Regularization may be employed in these cases. In regularization the likelihood function of the regression model is penalized for each effect modeled, thereby favoring a model with only a few effects (Efron et al., 2004). The penalty term in the function causes the coefficients to be shrunken toward zero, so that even if every single regression effect is modeled, only a few will be nonzero and thus retained in the final model.

Regularization can be used in the fitting of moderated nonlinear factor analysis (MNLFA) with a similar goal: to find only the DIF effects that are meaningful, in the absence of any a priori hypotheses about which effects are present (Bauer et al., 2020; Belzak & Bauer, 2020). If the unpenalized loglikelihood of the model is denoted *LL* and the vectors of intercept and loading DIF effects are denoted ν and Λ respectively, the penalized likelihood LL_{LASSO} can be obtained as follows:

$$LL_{LASSO} = LL - \tau \left(||\nu||_1 + ||\Lambda||_1 \right). \tag{24}$$

Here, τ is a tuning parameter which controls the extent to which parameters are shrunken toward zero, and $||x||_1$ represents the L1-norm of x. With non-zero values of τ, the loglikelihood function decreases when the absolute value of intercept and loading parameters increase. Thus, nonzero values of the DIF parameters will penalize the loglikelihood function. When the L1-norm is used, the penalty function is known as the least absolute shrinkage and selection operator (LASSO; Tibshirani, 1997). Other penalty functions can be used, including the L2-norm; this case is known as ridge regression. A flexible option is the elastic net penalty, which allows a combination of the L1-norm and L2-norm to be used as a penalty (Zou & Hastie, 2005); the relative weight of each norm is determined by a weighting parameter, typically denoted α.

Regularization-based methods solve some of the problems associated with specification search methods such as the ones described above. In particular, they eliminate the possibility that the order in which models are tested will affect the results of the final model. However, they are associated with a number of decisions. First, one must decide which penalty function to use, with options including LASSO, ridge regression, and elastic net, among others. If one uses elastic net, one must set the value of α, thereby deciding whether the L1- or L2-norm should be more heavily weighted. Note that LASSO and ridge regression are special cases of elastic net, which essentially applies both penalties in an adjustable proportion. Setting these values may lead to more or less sensitive tests, and therefore more or fewer DIF parameters retained. In all cases, one must set the value of τ, which sets the magnitude of the penalty function. Larger values of τ will lead to a greater penalty for additional effects, and therefore fewer DIF effects identified.

7.4.2 Alignment

Another approximate invariance method is alignment. This method, which has both frequentist and Bayesian implementations (Asparouhov & Muthén, 2014; Lai et al., 2021; Muthén & Asparouhov, 2018), takes advantage of the fact that there are infinitely many factor models with the same number of parameter constraints and the same level of fit. The algorithmm is mathematically complex, and the reader is encouraged to consult the work which introduced the alignment method (Asparouhov & Muthén, 2014; Muthén & Asparouhov, 2018) if they are interested in these details. However, the concept is explained here, with the hope that the benefits and general logic of the practice make sense even if the equations might require more context to fully understand.

Much like regularization, alignment provides estimates of DIF parameters without the analyst specifying any constraints a priori. The logic of this algorithm, which is quite similar to that of rotation within exploratory factor analysis, is to impose a simplicity constraint on the models which minimizes the number of measurement parameters that differ across groups (Asparouhov & Muthén, 2014). The first step of the algorithm is to estimate a configurally invariant model – that is, one in which all measurement parameters are allowed to vary freely even though the overall structure is the same – fixing factor means to 0 and factor variances to 1 for all factors, in all groups. Note that these constraints on the means and variances are required to identify the model. However, alignment takes advantage of the fact that there are infinitely many other constraints that we could use. So, after estimating the configural model, the alignment algorithm aims to fit a model with the exact same amount of constraints, and therefore the exact same fit, as the configural model. However, instead of constraining the means and variances of the factors, it estimates them freely, imposing the following constraints:

$$\lambda_{jg.aligned} = \frac{\lambda_{jg.configural}}{\sqrt{\psi_g.aligned}} \tag{25}$$

$$\nu_{jg.aligned} = \nu_{jg.configural} - \alpha_{g.aligned}\frac{\lambda_{jg.configural}}{\sqrt{\psi_g.aligned}}. \tag{26}$$

It then chooses values of latent variable means $\alpha_{g.aligned}$ and $\psi_{g.aligned}$ which yield values of $\lambda_{jg.aligned}$ and $\nu_{jg.aligned}$ that minimize the following function:

$$F = \sum_p \sum_{g<h} w_{g,h} f\left(\lambda_{jg.aligned} - \lambda_{jh.aligned}\right) + \sum_p \sum_{g<h} w_{g,h} f\left(\nu_{jg.aligned} - \nu_{jh.aligned}\right), \tag{27}$$

where $w_{g,h}$ is a weighting function based on the sizes of groups g and h. Additionally, $f(x)$ is a loss function. There are many values of this loss function we could use, and in general $f(x)$ is directly proportional to x (Asparouhov & Muthén, 2014). What the above simplicity constraint essentially implies is that, for each pair of groups g and h, alignment aims to choose values of latent variable means and variances which minimize the differences between the groups' loadings $\lambda_{jg.aligned}$ and intercepts $\nu_{jg.aligned}$. Thus, the goal of alignment is to retain a relatively small number of large invariance effects, minimizing most differences in parameters. One noted advantage of alignment is that it can be used with large numbers of groups (e.g., as many as 60; Marsh et al., 2018), because the simplicity function is a weighted combination of the pairwise differences between all groups.

7.4.3 Findings and Recommendations

Empirical findings about the robustness of regularization and alignment methods are fewer and further between than the other methods, given the relative novelty of these strategies. Here too, however, one must be guided first by the type of data and model with which one is working: whereas regularization can accommodate multiple covariates of any scale, alignment is to our knowledge only for groups. Because of the method's strong performance with large numbers of groups, one could simply make many groups from combinations of continuous variables; however, this method has not been tried to our knowledge.

Given the relative novelty of these methods, there are fewer concrete guidelines (relative to model-based methods) as to how best to employ them. Recommendations about the sample size required for both methods are tentative. The performance of alignment differs based on whether the latent variable mean α is estimated freely (currently parameterized as FREE in Mplus) or fixed to zero (currently parameterized as FIXED in Mplus), with the latter performing adequately with within-group sample sizes as low as $N = 100$, as long as the number of groups is small (Asparouhov & Muthén, 2014; Marsh et al., 2018). For regularization, there is some evidence that adequate performance can be achieved a total sample size as low as $N = 500$, provided DIF is large and relatively few items have DIF (Bauer et al., 2020).

In general, the success of the alignment method appears to be at least partially related to the number of groups and the proportion of noninvariant items (Flake & McCoach, 2018; Kim et al., 2017; Marsh et al., 2018). Alignment appears to yield the most accurate parameter estimates when the percentage of noninvariant items is relatively low (20–30%), consistent with some suggesting the use of the method when 25 percent or fewer of the items are noninvariant (Asparouhov & Muthén, 2014). By contrast, regularization appears to be particularly useful when the number of noninvariant items is large, showing considerably lower Type I error rates than standard model comparison approaches under high levels of noninvariance (Belzak & Bauer, 2020). However, these approximate invariance methods have not been compared to one another, and more work is needed to compare either method to pre-estimation methods and specification searches.

7.5 Effect Size Measures

All of the methods considered thus far are methods for determining whether DIF is present. A separate but related question is how large these DIF effects are. Some of the methods discussed in the preceding section, regularization and alignment, are premised on the idea that not all DIF effects are large enough to be meaningful and thus worthy of inclusion in the model. To this end, we need *effect size* measures for DIF, which are not necessarily DIF-locating strategies, per se. Rather, they are indices of the magnitude of DIF, which help us to determine the extent of its effect on individual items or the test as a whole. The last part of this section focuses on these measures. Although we have aimed to be comprehensive, note that there are a number of reviews which consider this topic in more detail (Chalmers, 2023; Gunn et al., 2020; Steinberg & Thissen, 2006). However, we include some discussion of effect sizes here because such measures are critical to our understanding of how to quantify the extent to which measurement invariance truly matters (Putnick et al., 2016).

As noted above, DIF is generally modeled as differences between measurement parameters such as λ_j, ν_j, and τ_{jk}. It is important to note that differences between groups in these parameter estimates are, in a sense, effect sizes: we can get a sense of the magnitude of DIF on each item simply by comparing parameter values. However, the magnitude of such measures do not tell the whole story about differences in measurement. In combination, certain values of λ_j, ν_j, and τ_j, even though they might be large numerically, may imply trace lines that are not far apart. Moreover, in the case of trace lines that cross, it is often the case that differences between groups at either end of the latent variable effectively cancel one another out – so although the response functions for each group diverge from one another, they do not consistently favor or disfavor either group. A quantity which captures this phenomenon is sometimes referred to as *compensatory DIF*. Following one recent review (Chalmers, 2023), we could term the magnitude of compensatory DIF on an item β_C, which is calculated as:

$$\beta_C = \int \left[E\left(y_{ij}|\eta_i, G = 0\right) - E\left(y_{ij}|\eta_i, G = 1\right) \right] f(\eta_i)\, d\eta_i. \qquad (28)$$

This is essentially the sum of all differences across η_i, both positive and negative, in the predicted response to y_{ij}. We can contrast this equation with the one for *noncompensatory DIF*, which is essentially the equation for all of the distance between the groups' trace lines, regardless of its direction. We can calculate an index of noncompensatory DIF, which we will term β_{NC} (Chalmers, 2023):

$$\beta_{NC}^2 = \int \left[E\left(y_{ij}|\eta_i, G = 0\right) - E\left(y_{ij}|\eta_i, G = 1\right) \right]^2 f(\eta_i)\, d\eta_i. \qquad (29)$$

We can take the square root of the entire expression (i.e., $\sqrt{\beta_{NC}^2}$), to get β_{NC}.

To understand what these two equations capture, we first notice that they consist of two main ingredients. The first is the difference between trace lines of the items – that is, $E\left(y_{ij}|\eta_i, G = 0\right) - E\left(y_{ij}|\eta_i, G = 0\right)$. The second is information about the distribution of the latent variable – that is, $f(\eta_i)$. The inclusion of $f(\eta_i)$ is important because, in some cases, large differences between trace lines may occur at portions of the latent variable distribution where very few respondents actually are. Consider, for instance, the possibility of two trace lines which diverge at values of η_i that are 3 standard deviations from the mean. Although there may be a divergence, and it may be a large one, it is likely not to be a particularly consequential one because it applies to very few individuals in the sample.

We now notice the way in which the two equations differ from one another: whereas the equation for β_C permits both positive and negative values, corresponding to either positive or negative differences between the trace lines, β_{NC}^2 does not because the difference term is squared. Thus, β_C can be referred to as a *signed* measure, and β_{NC} can be referred to as an *unsigned* measure.

In addition to item-level statistics, we can capture the overall burden of DIF on an entire test. The overall amount of difference in measurement parameters across all of a test's items is sometimes referred to as *differential test functioning* (DTF). Rather than dealing with item-level expected values, we can instead calculate the expected value of the score of the test, termed S_i for participant i at each value of the latent variable η_i (Stark et al., 2004). The trace line for this value is referred to as the *test characteristic curve*. We can calculate DTF as:

$$DTF = \int \left[E\left(S_i|\eta_i, G = 0\right) - E\left(S_i|\eta_i, G = 1\right) \right] f(\eta_i)\, d\eta_i. \tag{30}$$

Here $E\left(S_i|\eta_i, G = 0\right)$ and $E\left(S_i|\eta_i, G = 1\right)$ represent the test characteristic curves for groups 0 and 1, respectively. As mentioned earlier, we incorporate the distribution function for the latent variable, $f(\eta_i)$, which serves to weight the different portions of the test characteristic curve so that differences occurring at more frequent values of the latent variable receive more weight.

There are a wide variety of effect size measures that all aim to capture some estimate of the DIF and DTF measures given in Equations 28–30. They differ from one another in how they do so. Interestingly, the value of $\hat{\beta}$ given by Equation 23 when describing the SIBTEST procedure is one such estimate; that is, we could directly interpret the magnitude of $\hat{\beta}$ itself as an effect size measure.

Other measures approach the problem of finding β_C and β_{NC} by actually obtaining estimates of measurement parameters (i.e., $\hat{\lambda}$, $\hat{\nu}$, and, where relevant, $\hat{\tau}$) and plug these values into Equations 28–29 to obtain values of the expected values of y_{ij} under each group. One such measure is the weighted area between the curves (wABC) measure, which uses numerical integration to calculate the distance between trace lines for binary and ordinal variables (Edelen et al., 2015). However, there are a variety of other ways to do this, as well as a variety of other ways to approximate the distribution of η_i, as well as different ways of scaling the effect size. These differences affect the interpretation of these indices, as well as benchmark values to which they must be compared; for instance, whereas wABC values between 0.3 and 0.4 have been suggested as minimum criteria for considering removing an item due to DIF, other traceline-based measures have different numerical ranges and scales.

For continuous items, there is an added issue of how to scale estimates of β_C and β_{NC}, in order to obtain comparable estimates of the level of noninvariance across items of different scales (e.g., comparing a 12-point item to a 100-point one). One frequently used statistic is the dMACS (Nye & Drasgow, 2011), which is frequently used for continuous items. There are a number of similar measures for different types of items which make a variety of adjustments; though we will not write out the equations for these, we will compare and contrast them as well.

The dMACS is calculated as follows:

$$dMACS = \frac{1}{SD_{JP}} \sqrt{\int \left[E\left(y_{ij}|\eta_i, G=1\right) - E\left(y_{ij}|\eta_i, G=2\right) \right]^2 f(\eta_i)\, d\eta_i}. \quad (31)$$

Here, SD_{JP} is the standard deviation of item y_{ij}, pooled across the two groups as follows:

$$SD_{JP} = \frac{(N_1 - 1)\, SD_1 + (N_2 - 1)\, SD_1}{(N_1 - 1) + (N_2 - 1)}. \quad (32)$$

where N_1, N_2, SD_1, and SD_2 are the sample sizes and standard deviations of groups 1 and 2, respectively.

Note that this is an unsigned version of the dMACS, as squaring the differences between groups means that dMACS will always be positive. In other words, it is an estimate of β_{NC}. Additionally, recent work (Nye et al., 2019) proposes a signed version of the dMACS, termed $dMACS_{signed}$, which is given by:

$$dMACS_{signed} = \frac{1}{SD_{JP}} \int \left[E\left(y_{ij}|\eta_i, G=1\right) - E\left(y_{ij}|\eta_i, G=2\right) \right] f(\eta_i)\, d\eta_i. \quad (33)$$

Finally, as mentioned above, all of the possible effect sizes discussed here contain some way to incorporate information about the distribution of the latent variable, $f(\eta_i)$. However, the choice of how to approximate this distribution is a challenging one, because it is unclear which group's distribution to use. For instance, we could use the entire distribution across both groups, $f(\eta_i)$, by averaging the distribution functions of the groups. More often, however, there is a "focal" group – that is, a group whose potential noninvariance is of interest – which is being compared to a "reference" group. In this case, one chooses the distribution of η_i under either of these groups – either $f(\eta_i|G = 0)$ or $f(\eta_i|G = 1)$ – based on our questions (Gunn et al., 2020). Additionally, particularly with indices for binary and ordinal variables, there are a number of different ways to numerically approximate the distribution $f(\eta_i)$ – for example, by presuming a normal distribution, or by semiparametrically approximating the distribution based on the observed scores. Two recent reviews (Chalmers, 2023; Gunn et al., 2020) provide a number of alternative indices which are normalized with respect to different groups, and which use different methods of estimating $f(\eta_i)$, and give the rationale behind using each of them.

7.5.1 Findings and Recommendations

All of these effect sizes share at least one drawback: because they are based on differences between groups, they are incompatible with anything other than a multiple-groups formulation. If one is using a regression-based approach with continuous response variables, the only choice is to pick values of the covariates x_{ip} on which to form groups. Once groups have been formed, the consideration of which effect size measure to use comes down to the type of items one is considering. As noted above and in Table 5, continuous and binary/ordinal items are best served by different indices; the reader is referred to comprehensive overviews of measures for continuous (Gunn et al., 2020) and binary or ordinal (Chalmers, 2023) items. Beyond this, the results suggest that the choice of which index to use may come down to the predicted difference between groups in the latent variable means (Chalmers, 2023; Gunn et al., 2020). Because indices differ from one another in how the distribution of $f(\eta_i)$ is estimated, one must choose an index which is appropriately sensitive to the differences that actually exist between the groups. Additionally we suggest calculating one unsigned and one signed version of the same statistic and comparing them (Chalmers et al., 2016; Chalmers, 2023). If the two are substantially different from one another, this may provide insight into the nature of the differences between groups.

8 Recommendations for Best Practices

As has hopefully been demonstrated, there are not only many ways to test for measurement invariance or DIF but different ways to conceptualize these questions in the first place. Critically, we did not even consider a number of questions that are at the cutting edge of this rapidly advancing science. This omission includes (but is not limited to) Bayesian methods for testing and quantifying measurement invariance and DIF (e.g., Shi et al., 2019; Zhang et al., 2022), as well as whether and how measurement invariance can be considered in a network psychometric perspective (Epskamp et al., 2017). Another important area we have not discussed is a class of models which do not require the researcher to specify a priori which covariates are responsible for DIF. These approaches, which have a long history dating back to at least the 1990s, use mixture modeling to investigate heterogeneity in measurement parameters across unobserved subgroups, allowing a data-driven approach to determining whether and where DIF is present (Lubke & Neale, 2008; Rost, 1990). We have foregone discussion of these strategies focusing instead on cases in which the covariates of interest (or at least a number of suitable candidates) are known in advance.

If nothing else, these omissions should underscore to the reader that there is no one "right" way to study measurement invariance. A few recommendations follow from this, but they pertain more to broad decisions a researcher might make (e.g., whether to test for specific effects or use one of the data-driven algorithms discussed above), rather than specific methods to use. Our recommendations are as follows.

8.1 Always Visualize the Data before Doing Any Analyses.

As discussed above, visualizing the data helps the researcher to get a preliminary sense of whether item response patterns differ across individuals. This step can also help to identify problems with the data which need to be rectified before continuing. As discussed above, sparse response categories are well-known to cause problems with estimation in models for binary and ordinal data in general (DiStefano et al., 2021; Flora & Curran, 2004). With respect to measurement invariance in particular, the relatively high Type I error rates of some of the tests discussed above (e.g., some of the standard specification search approaches; (Belzak & Bauer, 2020; Woods, 2008), it is highly plausible that some tests will pick up on idiosyncrasies of the data, if present. If, for instance, a sparse response category is endorsed by participants at one level of the covariate (e.g., there are only five male participants and four of them endorsed an extreme response option), this may masquerade as a DIF effect which is likely an eccentric feature of the dataset.

We suggest undertaking as many exploratory, visual analyses as is feasible before fitting any models. We gave a few examples in Figures 4–6 of how researchers might go about this. However, others present comprehensive guides to premodeling data visualization steps which will help researchers to determine whether measurement invariance analyses will run into problems, as well as whether they may yield particularly useful information, in their dataset (Curran et al., 2014; Gottfredson et al., 2019).

8.2 Run as Many DIF Analyses as You Can and Report the Results Transparently.

Most of the algorithms above involve making some decisions, which may at times seem arbitrary in the sense that there are many other decisions that could be made at each step. For instance, the automated moderated nonlinear factor analysis (aMNLFA) algorithm mentioned above (Gottfredson et al., 2019) entails testing the effect of all P covariates on each item at once, which is effectively generalizing the likelihood ratio test (IRT-LR-DIF) to a mutiple-covariate case. Why not use the multiple-group factor analytic approach instead, testing the effect of a single covariate on the intercepts or loadings of all J items at once? Even if one accepts all of the steps in this algorithm as written, there are still a number of decisions the researcher must make. First, if one is working with an ordinal item, one must decide whether to test covariate effects on each individual item's thresholds (i.e., allowing DIF effects of each covariate in Equation 14) or to simply allow covariate effects on the overall intercept (i.e., constraining τ_{ikj} to equality in Equation 14 but allowing v_{ij} to differ across covariates). One must also decide what to do if estimation issues arise; these issues, such as empirical underidentification and model nonconvergence, are common to heavily parameterized models such moderated nonlinear factor analysis.

Even outside of specification searches, which may be particularly vulnerable to capitalizing on chance, each of the above methods entails some decisions. The pretest methods and effect sizes all have multiple variants (e.g., the different effects discussed by Chalmers (2023); Gunn et al. (2020)). Regularization (Belzak, 2020; Belzak & Bauer, 2020) requires the researcher to set the values of each tuning parameter. Similarly, in alignment (Asparouhov & Muthén, 2014; Muthén & Asparouhov, 2018), the researcher must make a number of decisions about how to formulate the loss function, which may have substantial effects on the ultimate solution.

The point of explicitly naming all of these choices is to emphasize that there are many researcher degrees of freedom in the modeling of measurement invariance. Moreover, no one method is "right." Although there is some evidence that the methods are differentially affected by certain nuances of each dataset (e.g., alignment being more adversely affected by larger proportions of noninvariant items), the reality is that much of what makes one method superior or inferior to another in a given circumstance is unknown. Researchers are therefore advised not to accept any one solution as the final word on the presence or absence of DIF but instead test multiple different methods and conclude whether and where DIF exists based on which effects appear repeatedly across methods. Moreover, we suggest reporting as many results as possible, making liberal use of online appendices and, when possible, posting the results of extra DIF analyses on OSF (https://osf.io/).

This logic also extends to our next and final point.

8.3 Do Not Substantively Interpret Data-Driven Findings

Most of the above methods for testing measurement invariance are essentially data-driven: the researcher comes in with no a priori hypotheses, and instead conducts some exhaustive search to determine what effects are present. Although each of the models shown above treats a given DIF effect as either a difference in parameters (in the multiple groups framework) or a parameter unto itself (in the regression framework), one should be careful about concluding that a test is "truly" noninvariant or an item "truly" has DIF from a given covariate. As has been noted before, DIF effects, particularly small DIF effects, may in many cases merely be artifacts of the sample (Steenkamp & Baumgartner, 1998). Of course, if one has hypotheses going into an analysis which are based in theory, it may make sense to consider the results of measurement invariance testing in light of these hypotheses. For instance, in the paper on anxiety symptoms among children with ASD cited at the beginning of this Element (Schiltz & Magnus, 2021), the authors clearly had theoretically driven reasons to believe that a core feature of ASD, social skills deficits, would adversely impact the functioning of the scale in specific ways. They justify these hypotheses, point out the respects in which their results are inconsistent with them, and do not overinterpret the effects that they found.

Absent strong hypotheses, we recommend testing for DIF with the goal of eliminating or accommodating it, not interpreting it. Much of the reason for this is the instability of DIF parameter estimates from one analysis to the next. We have recently examined the effects of small, seemingly arbitrary decisions on measurement-related findings, particularly in the context of data synthesis, using a multiverse analysis (Cole et al., 2022). By analyzing the same dataset 72 different times, each time using different variants of automated moderated nonlinear factor analysis and regularization as well as subtle differences in data management, we found substantial differences across analyses in the pattern and nature of DIF effects found. Substantively interpreting those findings would have been quite dangerous, as (1) we did not set out with any particular hypotheses as to the effect of our background variables on the items, and (2) many of these putative findings disappeared when slightly different analytic decisions were made.

Moreover, if one were guided by hypothesis tests of measurement invariance and DIF, one might conclude that an effect is present when, in reality, it is of such trivial magnitude as to be basically absent. In that spirit, the other major finding of the above-cited study (Cole et al., 2022) is that, even when DIF effects differed substantially across two models, they often produced very similar factor scores – that is, while DIF parameters were highly unstable, the factor scores which resulted from models with DIF were not. This finding corroborates those reported by other studies which have shown that even substantial DIF in terms of parameter estimates may lead to very few differences in factor scores (Chalmers et al., 2016; Curran et al., 2018). Instead of interpreting DIF effects themselves, we suggest interpreting DIF in terms of its effects on latent variable parameter estimates, item endorsement rates, and factor scores. The effect size metrics introduced above are very useful tools for doing exactly this (Chalmers, 2023; Gunn et al., 2020). Researchers should also run multiple different models and, in addition to determining which parameters hold up across multiple models, they should calculate the correlations among the factor scores generated by these models. If the correlations are high even when models themselves differ, that may strengthen one's confidence in the factor scores and (in our view, appropriately) weaken one's confidence in the meaning of the DIF parameters. Another potentially useful strategy is to obtain factor scores from a model without any DIF at all (i.e., a standard IRT or CFA model) and calculate the correlation between these factor scores and those resulting from a model which accounted for DIF effects, such as the multiple groups or regression-based models shown here.

The critical point to note, however, is that DIF does not need to be interpretable for it to be important. Whether or not we can generate an explanation for why a DIF effect may have appeared, the knowledge that it is present empowers us to take action – either by using a different scale, generating factor scores using a model which accounts for DIF, dropping an offending item, or doing whatever else might be necessary to make sure that every participant is measured fairly.

References

Asparouhov, T., & Muthén, B. (2014). Multiple-group factor analysis alignment. *Structural Equation Modeling: A Multidisciplinary Journal*, *21*(4), 495–508.

Bauer, D. J. (2017). A more general model for testing measurement invariance and differential item functioning. *Psychological Methods*, *22*(3), 507–526. https://doi.org/10.1037/met0000077.

Bauer, D. J., Belzak, W. C. M., & Cole, V. T. (2020). Simplifying the assessment of measurement invariance over multiple background variables: Using regularized moderated nonlinear factor analysis to detect differential item functioning. *Structural Equation Modeling*, *27*(1), 43–55. https://doi.org/10.1080/10705511.2019.1642754.

Bauer, D. J., & Hussong, A. M. (2009). Psychometric approaches for developing commensurate measures across independent studies: Traditional and new models. *Psychological Methods*, *14*(2), 101–125. https://doi.org/10.1037/a0015583.

Belzak, W. C. M. (2020). Testing differential item functioning in small samples. *Multivariate Behavioral Research*, *55*(5), 722–747. https://doi.org/10.1080/00273171.2019.1671162.

Belzak, W. C. M., & Bauer, D. J. (2020). Improving the assessment of measurement invariance: Using regularization to select anchor items and identify differential item functioning. *Psychological Methods*, *25*(6), 673–690. https://doi.org/10.1037/met0000253.

Bentler, P. M. (1990). Comparative fit indexes in structural models. *Psychological Bulletin*, *107*(2), 238.

Birmaher, B., Khetarpal, S., Brent, D., et al. (1997). The screen for child anxiety related emotional disorders (SCARED): Scale construction and psychometric characteristics. *Journal of the American Academy of Child & Adolescent Psychiatry*, *36*(4), 545–553.

Birnbaum, A. (1969). Statistical theory for logistic mental test models with a prior distribution of ability. *Journal of Mathematical Psychology*, *6*(2), 258–276.

Bock, R. D., & Zimowski, M. F. (1997). Multiple group IRT. In Linden, W. J., & Hambleton, R. K., (eds.), *Handbook of modern item response theory* (pp. 433–448). Springer.

Bollen, K. A. (1989). Structural equations with latent variables (Vol. 210). John Wiley & Sons.

Bond, T., Yan, Z., & Heene, M. (2020). *Applying the Rasch model: Fundamental measurement in the human sciences*. Routledge.

Brannick, M. T. (1995). Critical comments on applying covariance structure modeling. *Journal of Organizational Behavior, 16*(3), 201–213.

Byrne, B. M., Shavelson, R. J., & Muthén, B. (1989). Testing for the equivalence of factor covariance and mean structures: The issue of partial measurement invariance. *Psychological Bulletin, 105*(3), 456–466.

Chalmers, R. P. (2023). A unified comparison of IRT-based effect sizes for DIF investigations. *Journal of Educational Measurement, 60*(2), 318–350.

Chalmers, R. P., Counsell, A., & Flora, D. B. (2016). It might not make a big DIF: Improved differential test functioning statistics that account for sampling variability. *Educational and Psychological Measurement, 76*(1), 114–140.

Chang, H.-H., & Mazzeo, J. (1994). The unique correspondence of the item response function and item category response functions in polytomously scored item response models. *Psychometrika, 59*(3), 391–404.

Chen, F. F. (2007). Sensitivity of goodness of fit indexes to lack of measurement invariance. *Structural Equation Modeling: A Multidisciplinary Journal, 14*(3), 464–504.

Chen, F. F. (2008). What happens if we compare chopsticks with forks? The impact of making inappropriate comparisons in cross-cultural research. *Journal of Personality and Social Psychology, 95*(5), 1005–1018. https://doi.org/10.1037/a0013193.

Cheung, G. W., & Rensvold, R. B. (1999). Testing factorial invariance across groups: A reconceptualization and proposed new method. *Journal of Management, 25*(1), 1–27.

Cheung, G. W., & Rensvold, R. B. (2002a). Evaluating goodness-of-fit indexes for testing measurement invariance. *Structural Equation Modeling, 9*(2), 233–255.

Cheung, G. W., & Rensvold, R. B. (2002b). Evaluating goodness-of-fit indexes for testing measurement invariance. *Structural Equation Modeling, 9*(2), 233–255. https://doi.org/10.1207/s15328007sem0902_5.

Cohen, D. J., Dibble, E., & Grawe, J. M. (1977). Parental style: Mothers' and fathers' perceptions of their relations with twin children. *Archives of General Psychiatry, 34*(4), 445–451.

Cole, V. T., Hussong, A. M., Gottfredson, N. C., Bauer, D. J., & Curran, P. J. (2022). Informing harmonization decisions in integrative data analysis: Exploring the measurement multiverse. *Prevention Science*, 1–13.

Curran, P. J., Cole, V., Bauer, D. J., Hussong, A. M., & Gottfredson, N. (2016). Improving factor score estimation through the use of observed background characteristics. *Structural Equation Modeling: A Multidisciplinary Journal*, *23*(6), 827–844.

Curran, P. J., Cole, V. T., Bauer, D. J., Rothenberg, W. A., & Hussong, A. M. (2018). Recovering predictor–criterion relations using covariate-informed factor score estimates. *Structural Equation Modeling: A Multidisciplinary Journal*, *25*(6), 860–875.

Curran, P. J., McGinley, J. S., Bauer, D. J., et al. (2014). A moderated nonlinear factor model for the development of commensurate measures in integrative data analysis. *Multivariate Behavioral Research*, *49*(3), 214–231.

DeMars, C. E. (2009). Modification of the Mantel-Haenszel and logistic regression dif procedures to incorporate the sibtest regression correction. *Journal of Educational and Behavioral Statistics*, *34*(2), 149–170.

DiStefano, C., Shi, D., & Morgan, G. B. (2021). Collapsing categories is often more advantageous than modeling sparse data: Investigations in the CFA framework. *Structural Equation Modeling: A Multidisciplinary Journal*, *28*(2), 237–249.

DiStefano, C., Zhu, M., & Mindrila, D. (2009). Understanding and using factor scores: Considerations for the applied researcher. *Practical assessment, Research, and Evaluation*, *14*(1), 1–14. https://scholarworks.umass.edu/cgi/viewcontent.cgi?article=1226&context=pare.

Dorans, N. J., & Kulick, E. (1986). Demonstrating the utility of the standardization approach to assessing unexpected differential item performance on the scholastic aptitude test. *Journal of Educational Measurement*, *23*(4), 355–368.

Edelen, M. O., Stucky, B. D., & Chandra, A. (2015). Quantifying 'problematic' DIF within an IRT framework: Application to a cancer stigma index. *Quality of Life Research*, *24*, 95–103.

Efron, B., Hastie, T., Johnstone, I., & Tibshirani, R. (2004). Least angle regression. *The Annals of Statistics*, *32*(2), 407–499.

Epskamp, S., Rhemtulla, M., & Borsboom, D. (2017). Generalized network psychometrics: Combining network and latent variable models. *Psychometrika*, *82*(4), 904–927.

Ferrando, P. J. (2002). Theoretical and empirical comparisons between two models for continuous item response. *Multivariate Behavioral Research*, *37*(4), 521–542.

Finch, H. (2005). The MIMIC model as a method for detecting DIF: Comparison with Mantel–Haenszel, SIBTEST, and the IRT likelihood ratio. *Applied Psychological Measurement*, *29*(4), 278–295.

Fischer, H. F., & Rose, M. (2019). Scoring depression on a common metric: A comparison of EAP estimation, plausible value imputation, and full Bayesian IRT modeling. *Multivariate Behavioral Research*, *54*(1), 85–99.

Flake, J. K., & McCoach, D. B. (2018). An investigation of the alignment method with polytomous indicators under conditions of partial measurement invariance. *Structural Equation Modeling: A Multidisciplinary Journal*, *25*(1), 56–70.

Flora, D. B., & Curran, P. J. (2004). An empirical evaluation of alternative methods of estimation for confirmatory factor analysis with ordinal data. *Psychological Methods*, *9*(4), 466–491.

French, B. F., & Finch, W. H. (2006). Confirmatory factor analytic procedures for the determination of measurement invariance. *Structural Equation Modeling*, *13*(3), 378–402. https://doi.org/10.1207/s153 28007sem1303_3.

Gottfredson, N. C., Cole, V. T., Giordano, M. L., et al. (2019). Simplifying the implementation of modern scale scoring methods with an automated R package: Automated moderated nonlinear factor analysis (AMNLFA). *Addictive Behaviors*, 94, 65–73.

Gray, M., & Sanson, A. (2005). Growing up in Australia: The longitudinal study of Australian children. *Family Matters*, (72), 4–9.

Grice, J. W. (2001). Computing and evaluating factor scores. *Psychological Methods*, *6*(4), 430.

Gunn, H. J., Grimm, K. J., & Edwards, M. C. (2020). Evaluation of six effect size measures of measurement non-invariance for continuous outcomes. *Structural Equation Modeling*, *27*(4), 503–514. https://doi.org/10.1080 /10705511.2019.1689507.

Holland, P. W., & Thayer, D. T. (1986). Differential item functioning and the Mantel–Haenszel procedure. *ETS Research Report Series*, *1986*(2), i–24.

Horn, J. L., & McArdle, J. J. (1992). A practical and theoretical guide to measurement invariance in aging research. *Experimental Aging Research*, *18*(3), 117–144.

Hosmer Jr, D. W., Lemeshow, S., & Sturdivant, R. X. (2013). *Applied Logistic Regression* (Vol. 398). John Wiley.

Hoyle, R. H. (1995). *Structural equation modeling: Concepts, issues, and applications.* Sage.

Jiang, H., & Stout, W. (1998). Improved type I error control and reduced estimation bias for DIF detection using SIBTEST. *Journal of Educational and Behavioral Statistics, 23*(4), 291–322.

Jodoin, M. G., & Gierl, M. J. (2001). Evaluating type I error and power rates using an effect size measure with the logistic regression procedure for DIF detection. *Applied Measurement in Education, 14*(4), 329–349.

Jöreskog, K. G. (1971). Simultaneous factor analysis in several populations. *Psychometrika, 36*(4), 409–426.

Kim, E. S., Cao, C., Wang, Y., & Nguyen, D. T. (2017). Measurement invariance testing with many groups: A comparison of five approaches. *Structural Equation Modeling: A Multidisciplinary Journal, 24*(4), 524–544.

Knott, M., & Bartholomew, D. J. (1999). *Latent variable models and factor analysis* (Vol. 7). Edward Arnold.

Kopf, J., Zeileis, A., & Strobl, C. (2015a). Anchor selection strategies for DIF analysis: Review, assessment, and new approaches. *Educational and Psychological Measurement, 75*(1), 22–56.

Kopf, J., Zeileis, A., & Strobl, C. (2015b). A framework for anchor methods and an iterative forward approach for DIF detection. *Applied Psychological Measurement, 39*(2), 83–103.

Lai, M. H., Liu, Y., & Tse, W. W. Y. (2022). Adjusting for partial invariance in latent parameter estimation: Comparing forward specification search and approximate invariance methods. *Behavior Research Methods, 54*(1), 414–434. https://doi.org/10.3758/s13428-021-01560-2.

Lai, M. H. C., & Zhang, Y. (2022). Classification accuracy of multidimensional tests: Quantifying the impact of noninvariance. *Structural Equation Modeling: A Multidisciplinary Journal, 29*(4), 620–629, 1–10. https://doi.org/10.1080/10705511.2021.1977936.

Li, H.-H., & Stout, W. (1996). A new procedure for detection of crossing DIF. *Psychometrika, 61*(4), 647–677.

Li, Z., & Zumbo, B. D. (2009). Impact of differential item functioning on subsequent statistical conclusions based on observed test score data. *Psicológica, 30*(2), 343–370.

Lubke, G., & Neale, M. (2008). Distinguishing between latent classes and continuous factors with categorical outcomes: Class invariance of parameters of factor mixture models. *Multivariate Behavioral Research, 43*(4), 592–620.

MacCallum, R. C., Roznowski, M., & Necowitz, L. B. (1992). Model modifications in covariance structure analysis: The problem of capitalization on chance. *Psychological Bulletin*, *111*(3), 490–504.

Marsh, H. W., Guo, J., Parker, P. D., et al. (2018). What to do when scalar invariance fails: The extended alignment method for multi-group factor analysis comparison of latent means across many groups. *Psychological Methods*, *23*(3), 524–545.

Maydeu-Olivares, A., & Cai, L. (2006). A cautionary note on using g2 (DIF) to assess relative model fit in categorical data analysis. *Multivariate Behavioral Research*, *41*(1), 55–64.

McCullagh, P., & Nelder, J. A. (2019). *Generalized linear models*. Routledge.

McNeish, D., & Wolf, M. G. (2020). Thinking twice about sum scores. *Behavior Research Methods*, *52*(6), 2287–2305.

Meade, A. W., Johnson, E. C., & Braddy, P. W. (2008). Power and sensitivity of alternative fit indices in tests of measurement invariance. *Journal of Applied Psychology*, *93*(3), 568–592. https://doi.org/10.1037/0021-9010.93.3.568.

Meade, A. W., & Lautenschlager, G. J. (2004). A comparison of item response theory and confirmatory factor analytic methodologies for establishing measurement equivalence/invariance. *Organizational Research Methods*, *7*(4), 361–388. https://doi.org/10.1177/1094428104268027.

Meade, A. W., & Wright, N. A. (2012). Solving the measurement invariance anchor item problem in item response theory. *Journal of Applied Psychology*, *97*(5), 1016–1031. https://doi.org/10.1037/a0027934.

Mellenbergh, G. J. (1989). Item bias and item response theory. *International Journal of Educational Research*, *13*(2), 127–143. https://doi.org/10.1016/0883-*0355*(89)90002-5.

Meredith, W. (1993). Measurement invariance, factor analysis and factorial invariance. *Psychometrika*, *58*(4), 525–543.

Millsap, R. E. (1997). Invariance in measurement and prediction: Their relationship in the single-factor case. *Psychological Methods*, *2*(3), 248–260.

Millsap, R. E. (1998). Group differences in regression intercepts: Implications for factorial invariance. *Multivariate Behavioral Research*, *33*(3), 403–424.

Millsap, R. E. (2011). *Statistical approaches to measurement invariance*. Routledge. https://doi.org/10.4324/9780203821961.

Millsap, R. E., & Kwok, O.-M. (2004). Evaluating the impact of partial factorial invariance on selection in two populations. *Psychological Methods*, *9*(1), 93–115. https://doi.org/10.1037/1082-989x.9.1.93.

Millsap, R. E., & Meredith, W. (2007). Factorial invariance: Historical perspectives and new problems. In Cudeck, R., and MacCallum, R. C., (eds.), *Factor analysis at 100* (pp. 145–166). Routledge.

Millsap, R. E., & Yun-Tein, J. (2004). Assessing factorial invariance in ordered-categorical measures. *Multivariate Behavioral Research*, *39*(3), 479–515.

Muraki, E., & Engelhard Jr, G. (1985). Full-information item factor analysis: Applications of EAP scores. *Applied Psychological Measurement*, *9*(4), 417–430.

Muthén, B. O. (1989). Latent variable modeling in heterogeneous populations. *Psychometrika*, *54*(4), 557–585.

Muthén, B., & Asparouhov, T. (2018). Recent methods for the study of measurement invariance with many groups: Alignment and random effects. *Sociological Methods & Research*, *47*(4), 637–664.

Nye, C. D., Bradburn, J., Olenick, J., Bialko, C., & Drasgow, F. (2019). How big are my effects? Examining the magnitude of effect sizes in studies of measurement equivalence: *Organizational Research Methods*, *22*(3), 678–709. https://doi.org/10.1177/1094428118761122.

Nye, C. D., & Drasgow, F. (2011). Effect size indices for analyses of measurement equivalence: Understanding the practical importance of differences between groups. *Journal of Applied Psychology*, *96*(5), 966–980. https://doi.org/10.1037/a0022955.

Osterlind, S. J., & Everson, H. T. (2009). *Differential item functioning*. Sage.

Putnick, D. L., & Bornstein, M. H. (2016). Measurement invariance conventions and reporting: The state of the art and future directions for psychological research. *Developmental Review*, *41*(41), 71–90. https://doi.org/10.1016/j.dr.2016.06.004.

Raykov, T., Marcoulides, G. A., Harrison, M., & Zhang, M. (2020). On the dependability of a popular procedure for studying measurement invariance: A cause for concern? *Structural Equation Modeling: A Multidisciplinary Journal*, *27*(4), 649–656.

Reckase, M. D. (1997). The past and future of multidimensional item response theory. *Applied Psychological Measurement*, *21*(1), 25–36.

Reise, S. P., Widaman, K. F., & Pugh, R. H. (1993). Confirmatory factor analysis and item response theory: Two approaches for exploring measurement invariance. *Psychological Bulletin*, *114*(3), 552–566.

Rost, J. (1990). Rasch models in latent classes: An integration of two approaches to item analysis. *Applied Psychological Measurement*, *14*(3), 271–282.

Roussos, L. A., & Stout, W. F. (1996). Simulation studies of the effects of small sample size and studied item parameters on SIBTEST and Mantel–Haenszel type I error performance. *Journal of Educational Measurement*, *33*(2), 215–230.

Rutter, M., Bailey, A., & Lord, C. (2003). SCQ. *The Social Communication Questionnaire. Torrance, CA: Western Psychological Services.* https://www.wpspublish.com/store/p/2954/social-communication-questionnaire-scq.

Samejima, F. (1997). Graded response model. In Linden, W. J., & Hambleton, R. K., (eds.), *Handbook of modern item response theory* (pp. 85–100). Springer.

Sanson, A. V., Nicholson, J., Ungerer, J., et al. (2002). *Introducing the longitudinal study of Australian children.* Australian Institute of Family Studies.

Satorra, A., & Bentler, P. M. (2001). A scaled difference chi-square test statistic for moment structure analysis. *Psychometrika*, *66*(4), 507–514.

Satorra, A., & Saris, W. E. (1985). Power of the likelihood ratio test in covariance structure analysis. *Psychometrika*, *50*(1), 83–90.

Savalei, V., & Kolenikov, S. (2008). Constrained versus unconstrained estimation in structural equation modeling. *Psychological Methods*, *13*(2), 150–170.

Schiltz, H. K., & Magnus, B. E. (2021). Differential item functioning based on autism features, IQ, and age on the screen for child anxiety related disorders (SCARED) among youth on the autism spectrum. *Autism Research*, *14*(6), 1220–1236.

Schneider, L., Chalmers, R. P., Debelak, R., & Merkle, E. C. (2020). Model selection of nested and non-nested item response models using Vuong tests. *Multivariate Behavioral Research*, *55*(5), 664–684.

Shealy, R., & Stout, W. (1993). A model-based standardization approach that separates true bias/DIF from group ability differences and detects test bias/DTF as well as item bias/DIF. *Psychometrika*, *58*(2), 159–194.

Shi, D., Song, H., DiStefano, C., et al. (2019). Evaluating factorial invariance: An interval estimation approach using bayesian structural equation modeling. *Multivariate Behavioral Research*, *54*(2), 224–245. https://doi.org/10.1080/00273171.2018.1514484.

Skrondal, A., & Laake, P. (2001). Regression among factor scores. *Psychometrika*, 66, 563–575.

Skrondal, A., & Rabe-Hesketh, S. (2004). *Generalized latent variable modeling: Multilevel, longitudinal, and structural equation models.* Chapman Hall/CRC.

Stark, S., Chernyshenko, O. S., & Drasgow, F. (2004). Examining the effects of differential item (functioning and differential) test functioning on selection decisions: When are statistically significant effects practically important? *Journal of Applied Psychology, 89*(3), 497–508.

Stark, S., Chernyshenko, O. S., & Drasgow, F. (2006). Detecting differential item functioning with confirmatory factor analysis and item response theory: Toward a unified strategy. *Journal of Applied Psychology, 91*(6), 1292–1306.

Steenkamp, J.-B. E., & Baumgartner, H. (1998). Assessing measurement invariance in cross-national consumer research. *Journal of Consumer Research, 25*(1), 78–90.

Steiger, J. H. (1998). A note on multiple sample extensions of the RMSEA fit index. *Structural Equation Modeling, 5*(4), 411–419.

Steinberg, L., & Thissen, D. (2006). Using effect sizes for research reporting: Examples using item response theory to analyze differential item functioning. *Psychological Methods, 11*(4), 402–415.

Steinmetz, H. (2013). Analyzing observed composite differences across groups: Is partial measurement invariance enough? *Methodology: European Journal of Research Methods for the Behavioral and Social Sciences, 9*(1), 1–12.

Stoel, R. D., Garre, F. G., Dolan, C., & Van Den Wittenboer, G. (2006). On the likelihood ratio test in structural equation modeling when parameters are subject to boundary constraints. *Psychological Methods, 11*(4), 439–455.

Swaminathan, H., & Rogers, H. J. (1990). Detecting differential item functioning using logistic regression procedures. *Journal of Educational Measurement, 27*(4), 361–370.

Thissen, D. (2001). IRTLRDIF v. 2.0 b: Software for the computation of the statistics involved in item response theory likelihood-ratio tests for differential item functioning. Chapel Hill, NC: LL Thurstone Psychometric Laboratory.

Thissen, D., Steinberg, L., & Kuang, D. (2002). Quick and easy implementation of the Benjamini-Hochberg procedure for controlling the false positive rate in multiple comparisons. *Journal of Educational and Behavioral Statistics, 27*(1), 77–83.

Thissen, D., Steinberg, L., & Wainer, H. (1993). Detection of differential item functioning using the parameters of item response models. In Holland, P. W., & Wainer, H., (eds.), *Differential Item Functioning* (pp. 67–113). Lawrence Erlbaum Associates.

Tibshirani, R. (1997). The lasso method for variable selection in the Cox model. *Statistics in Medicine, 16*(4), 385–395.

Tucker, L. R., & Lewis, C. (1973). A reliability coefficient for maximum likelihood factor analysis. *Psychometrika*, 38, 1–10.

Vandenberg, R. J., & Lance, C. E. (2000). A review and synthesis of the measurement invariance literature: Suggestions, practices, and recommendations for organizational research. *Organizational Research Methods*, *3*(1), 4–70.

Vernon-Feagans, L., Willoughby, M., Garrett-Peters, P., & Family Life Project Key Investigators. (2016). Predictors of Behavioral Regulation in Kindergarten: Household Chaos, Parenting and Early Executive Functions. *Developmental Psychology*, *52*(3), 430.

Wachs, T. D. (2013). Relation of maternal personality to perceptions of environmental chaos in the home. *Journal of Environmental Psychology*, *34*, 1–9.

Wirth, R., & Edwards, M. C. (2007). Item factor analysis: Current approaches and future directions. *Psychological Methods*, *12*(1), 58–79.

Woods, C. M. (2008). IRT-LR-DIF with estimation of the focal-group density as an empirical histogram. *Educational and Psychological Measurement*, *68*(4), 571–586.

Woods, C. M. (2009a). Empirical selection of anchors for tests of differential item functioning. *Applied Psychological Measurement*, *33*(1), 42–57.

Woods, C. M. (2009b). Evaluation of MIMIC-model methods for DIF testing with comparison to two-group analysis. *Multivariate Behavioral Research*, *44*(1), 1–27.

Woods, C. M., Cai, L., & Wang, M. (2013). The Langer-improved Wald test for DIF testing with multiple groups: Evaluation and comparison to two-group IRT. *Educational and Psychological Measurement*, *73*(3), 532–547.

Xu, Y. & Green, S. B. (2016). The impact of varying the number of measurement invariance constraints on the assessment of between-group differences of latent means. *Structural equation modeling*, *23*(2), 290–301. https://doi.org/10.1080/10705511.2015.1047932.

Yoon, M., & Kim, E. S. (2014). A comparison of sequential and nonsequential specification searches in testing factorial invariance. *Behavior Research Methods*, *46*(4), 1199–1206. https://doi.org/10.3758/s13428-013-0430-2.

Yoon, M., & Millsap, R. E. (2007). Detecting violations of factorial invariance using data-based specification searches: A Monte Carlo study. *Structural Equation Modeling*, *14*(3), 435–463. https://doi.org/10.1080/10705510701301677.

Yuan, K.-H., & Bentler, P. M. (2004). On chi-square difference and z tests in mean and covariance structure analysis when the base model is misspecified. *Educational and Psychological Measurement*, *64*(5), 737–757.

Zhang, Y., Lai, M. H., & Palardy, G. J. (2022). A Bayesian region of measurement equivalence (ROME) approach for establishing measurement invariance. *Psychological Methods*, *28*(4), 993–1004.

Zou, H., & Hastie, T. (2005). Regularization and variable selection via the elastic net. *Journal of the Royal Statistical Society: Series B (Statistical Methodology)*, *67*(2), 301–320.

Zubrick, S. R., Lucas, N., Westrupp, E. M., & Nicholson, J. M. (2014). *Parenting Measures in the Longitudinal Study of Australian Children: Construct Validity and Measurement Quality, Waves 1 to 4*. Canberra: Department of social services 1–100.

Zwick, R. (1990). When do item response function and Mantel–Haenszel definitions of differential item functioning coincide? *Journal of Educational Statistics*, *15*(3), 185–197.

Acknowledgments

This Element uses unit record data from Growing Up in Australia: the Longitudinal Study of Australian Children (LSAC). LSAC is conducted by the Australian Government Department of Social Services (DSS). The findings and views reported in this Element, however, are those of the author[s] and should not be attributed to the Australian Government, DSS, or any of DSS' contractors or partners. DOI: 10.26193/QR4L6Q

Cambridge Elements ≡

Research Methods for Developmental Science

Brett Laursen
Florida Atlantic University

Brett Laursen is a Professor of Psychology at Florida Atlantic University. He is Editor-in-Chief of the *International Journal of Behavioral Development*, where he previously served as the founding Editor of the Methods and Measures section. Professor Laursen received his Ph.D. in Child Psychology from the Institute of Child Development at the University of Minnesota and an Honorary Doctorate from Örebro University, Sweden. He is a Docent Professor of Educational Psychology at the University of Helsinki, and a Fellow of the American Psychological Association (Division 7, Developmental), the Association for Psychological Science, and the International Society for the Study of Behavioural Development. Professor Laursen is the co-editor of the *Handbook of Developmental Research Methods* and the *Handbook of Peer Interactions, Relationships, and Groups*.

About the Series

Each offering in this series will focus on methodological innovations and contemporary strategies to assess adjustment and measure change, empowering scholars of developmental science who seek to optimally match their research questions to pioneering methods and quantitative analyses.

Cambridge Elements ≡

Research Methods for Developmental Science

Elements in the Series

Measurement Burst Designs to Improve Precision in Peer Research
Ryan J. Persram, Bianca Panarello, Melisa Castellanos, Lisa Astrologo and
William M. Bukowski

*Language Assessments for Preschool Children: Validity and Reliability of Two
New Instruments Administered by Childcare Educators*
Anders Højen, Dorthe Bleses and Philip S. Dale

*Parceling in Structural Equation Modeling: A Comprehensive Introduction for
Developmental Scientists*
Todd D. Little, Charlie Rioux, Omolola A. Odejimi and Zachary L. Stickley

*Identifying and Minimizing Measurement Invariance Among Intersectional
Groups: The Alignment Method Applied to Multi-category Items*
Rachel A. Gordon, Tianxiu Wang, Hai Nguyen and Ariel M. Aloe

Algorithms for Measurement Invariance Testing: Contrasts and Connections
Veronica T. Cole and Conor H. Lacey

A full series listing is available at www.cambridge.org/ERMD

Printed in the United States
by Baker & Taylor Publisher Services